Know Better, Do Better!

A Call to Wake up, Man up, and Rise up

(Seizing every opportunity God gave you)

_____

Elmo Overton
Know Better, Do Better

Copyright © 2019 by Elmo Overton

ISBN 978-1-54399-829-0

Printed in the USA

Impetus

Having to complete high school later in life because he had to leave school to support his family and not completing college, my father is probably the most unlikely person to write a book. Yet, he is the very person who should write a book. He has learned and succeeded through living, through taking risks, and through an unfailing belief that anything is possible. His belief in his children and grandchildren forms the foundation on which all of our successes are built.

Daughters, Monica and Mia

Preface

Losing my father at a young age and being born into poverty, I knew there were clearly only three paths that I could take. I could become a negative member of my community and engage in a life of crime and mischief; I could stay complacent and continue to live the life I was born into, barely making ends meet and living in the same community; or I could make a conscious effort to *do better* and to ensure that my children grow up financially more stable than I did.

This is not a how-to book. I am trying to sound the battle cry. We were never meant to be apathetic complainers or immature wimps. We were called to reach for greatness. I want to encourage the faint-hearted, the defeated, and the disinformed. Get your mind right, because this is a call to wake up, man up, and rise up. It is time for us to be the heads of our households, the role models for the younger generation, the registered voters, the leaders in our communities, and the property and business owners. We all have something in common. We want our children to do better in life than we did.

Know Better Do Better

This will take work. So, let me ask you one question. Are you willing to do the work that is required?

Introduction

Conquering Your Biggest Enemy

Romans 8:15: *For you did not receive the spirit of slavery to fall back into fear . . .*

Fear will try to stop you from chasing your dreams. And if fear can stop you from chasing, then fear can stop you from realizing your full potential. Let's say that you want to start your own business. You have been thinking about doing this for years. You may have even been doing it part time for years. But now you are at a crossroads, and it is time to make your move. You told yourself two or three years ago that it was time for you to move on to this business full time.

You take the first big step. You talk to your family and friends and tell them about your dream. Now, look what happens. You have just opened Pandora's box. Here come the naysayers, the critical, the jealous, the fearful, and the hard-hearted. They will tell you that the banks are not lending money to small businesses like they used to. They will tell you that they just don't want you to lose your hard-earned money.

Know Better Do Better

Others will say that you have a right to be slow and cautious about this dream, because unlike other people, your money did not come from an inheritance or from your rich uncle. Your money did not come from a gift or from an investment account at the bank. It was not a loan from Mom and Dad, nor was it from a court case settlement. For the most part, your money came from sacrificing and saving. It came from working overtime and weekends and holidays. It came from careful decision-making and keeping it out of the hands of those who may misuse it. These are just the things they will say to your face. And now, with the help of your family and friends, you have awakened your biggest enemy: fear. Mr. Fear will tell you everything that your naysayers and haters did not tell you. It will come at you from all directions. It will come at you day and night, even during those times when you are not working and are supposed to be having fun. It will persist until you finally pray for God to give you courage and help you to be strong. After that, even though fear may continue to stand right beside you, it will not be able to overpower you.

African Americans are the biggest consumers in this country. We buy everything, and yet, we own nothing. So, pursue that dream of owning a convenience store, or restaurant, or shoe store, or computer and phone repair shop. There are thousands and thousands of businesses that you could go into and make a better day for you and your family and those you will one day leave behind. If your haters think that buying a new car or house is the way to get ahead, let them continue to believe that. At the end of the day, you will achieve the success you desire, and they will still be trying to spend their way out of a financial hole. Pursue your dreams.

Chapter One

Deuteronomy 10:17: *For the Lord, your God is God of gods and the Lord of lords, the great God, mighty and awesome, who shows no partiality and accepts no bribes*

Black Community's Wounds

I recently read a book entitled *Captivating* by Stasi Eldridge. In her book, she discussed the concept of the "wound" that men and women share. The wound as she calls it is an emotional response to the areas of hurt in a person's life. She went on to say that while God designs our sufferings to build us up, Satan strategizes to have us define ourselves by our hurts instead of our victories. The author proposed that Satan's technique is to constantly create situations that affirm the hurt in a person's life so that instead of seeking to heal, the person begins to see themselves as beyond saving. On the other hand, God's design is to enter into that very place of hurt in order to deal with the situation appropriately and heal the hurt entirely. In the end, God intends the area of hurt to become an area of strength so that the personal victory can be a living testimony to others.

As I thought about this concept, I realized that the African American community has a wound. From the beginning of history here in America, our ancestors were told and treated as if their lives did not matter. Their families were split up and no one cared. The women were raped, and no one helped. Their lives were taken at will with no objection. After slavery ended and the reconstruction period began, African Americans sought to build cities, open colleges, run for offices, and start enterprises. Yet, within a very few years, Jim Crow began to cripple the dreams that had just begun to walk. The wound never healed. As time progressed, it seems that, instead of actively seeking to heal from the hurts inflicted on our community, we have begun to internalize these hurts and respond according to our defeats. It seems that, in some ways, we have developed a mentality that affirms the hurts and disregards our need for healing. The slave trade is no longer splitting up families, but we do it to ourselves when we continue to behave irresponsibly, or break the law and go to jail, or choose not to get married so we can continue to live off of the system. Slavery is no longer keeping African Americans from getting an education, but we keep it from ourselves when we choose not to learn, think it is cool to be dumb, bring violence into our schools, or drop out. Our women are no longer being demoralized by slave masters, but we demoralize ourselves by calling them hoes or actively participating in behaviors that make the statement true. There was a time when African Americans were called the N-word by white oppressors. Now we use that term when referring to one another. We no longer have the Klan waiting to harm us if we go to the polls and vote. We instead keep ourselves from the polls by being nonchalant and uninvolved. As if that were not bad enough, today we are seeing several instances of unarmed black men being killed at the hands of law enforcement officers. Yet, the real tragedy is that, for every instance of white on black crimes, there are ten instances of black on black crime where we have killed our own. Sadly, in both cases, chances are the killer will go free.

Let's change the subject for a moment. Let's talk about elephants. Elephants can weigh up to seven tons and are said to be as strong as hundred men. Yet they can be domesticated and owned like one would own a dog or a cat, all because of something I like to call the "Elephant Mentality." In this brief discussion about the "Elephant Mentality," we will learn exactly what it is and how it influences us today in the African American community.

So, let's begin at the most intriguing part: how people own elephants. The domestication of an elephant is actually surprisingly simple. Elephants are purchased when they are very young. They are chained in thick, inescapable chains. No matter how hard the young elephant pulls, it will not escape. In fact, trying to escape only causes the elephant pain, as the heavy chains tear into its tender skin. Once the elephant is fully grown, getting him to stay in one place is as simple as tying a string around his leg and using a stick to peg the string to the ground. To the casual observer, it would seem that the elephant is not chained at all. One flick of this magnificent creature's mighty leg and he is free, but he doesn't try. Why? Because in his mind, he is still in chains. He remembers the pain he experienced the last time he tried to be free, so he stays in domestication and bondage.

Know Better Do Better

So, what does this have to do with us in the African American community? It is clear that we are no longer bound in the chains of slavery or Jim Crow. It is clear from what we've already achieved that we can achieve exceedingly and abundantly. So why is it that so many of our young men drop out of high school and surrender to the chains of minimum wage? Why is it that so many of our young women would rather be mothers of children instead of mothers of success? Why is it that despite the hard work of people before us, so few of us are seen on top? Because like the elephant, our minds are still in chains.

It would be a lie to say that, as African Americans, we are often recipients of special opportunity or easy routes to achievement in this world. For us, success is something that is not easy but possible. It is our job to stop talking about how things are unfair. We need to stop discussing how the system is rigged to stop us from getting ahead. It is not enough to simply say we need to rise up. We must stop feeling sorry for ourselves and take steps toward actually rising up. We need to get out of the "Elephant Mentality." So how do we get out?

Romans 12:2 says, "Do not conform any longer to the pattern of this world but be transformed by the renewing of your mind. Then you will be able to test and approve what Gods will is. His good, pleasing and perfect will." Getting out of the "Elephant Mentality" is done by renewing our minds. The system is rigged, but those chains do not stop us from getting ahead. The current unfairness of our society is not a roadblock but a hindrance. If we focus on Gods' will for us, nothing will be able to stop us. Someone once said, "Cowards never start. The weak never finish. Winners never quit." We are winners, and until we reach our Christ-driven purpose, we must never quit.

Crime and Punishment

On the eve of Martin Luther King Luther Day, 2016, there appeared quite an interesting article in the *Virginian Pilot* written by Lillie Branch Kennedy, the founder of Resource Information Help for the Disadvantaged, and Quan Williams, a policy associate for the New Virginia Majority. Although this article was printed in my local newspaper, it reflects an idea that is common in most cities around the world. The article, entitled "The Arc of Virginia Justice," references a quote from a speech that Dr. King had given at Wesleyan University in 1964. "The arc of the moral universe is long but bends toward justice." According to the article, in 1995, Virginia Governor George Allen passed a series of laws called the "Truth in Sentencing" policy. Among other things, these policies abolished parole in Virginia, and yet did not require judges to tell jurors that parole was not an option. As a result, a disproportionate number of African Americans were sentenced to much harsher terms than they would have served, as the jurors did not know that it would be a mandatory and permanent sentence. This travesty of justice continued for five years until an inmate named Richard Fishback appealed his eighteen-year sentence to the state supreme court. It was only then that this Truth in Sentencing policy was brought to light and abolished. However, it was not retroactive for those already imprisoned, nor did it require that past jurors be alerted of their deception. Fishback was resentenced.

Now, sixteen years later, many inmates have served terms that their jurors never dreamed they would have to complete, and over five hundred others, sentenced during the years of 1995 and 2000, are still incarcerated.

A recent *Associated Press* story shares this problem through the eyes of juror Tom Tignor, who admits that the jury he served on would have recommended a shorter sentence had it known that there was no more parole. According to the ACLU, "African Americans remain more likely to receive harsher treatment at every stage of the criminal justice system, from stops on the street to sentencing, when compared to similar white defendants." Perhaps this point could not be made clearer than by the case of Daniel Richard Ford III. Ford was recommended for a six-and-half-year sentence for a drug offense. After the trial, however, the jury gave Ford over three hundred years. Later, the sentence was commuted to forty years, and Ford is not scheduled for release until 2034. I say again, forty years for a drug offense that would have only carried a six-year sentence for *someone else.*

Despite these staggering stories, there is hope that, one day, justice and truth will prevail. Current Virginia Governor Terry McAuliffe recently organized a twenty-seven-member commission on Parole Review. This commission is aimed at legislation to "provide an opportunity for sentence modification." It is my hope that one day King's dream of truth, equality, and color-blind justice will one day be realized in Virginia.

Opioid vs. Crack Addiction: A Racial Double Standard

Romans 12:1: I appeal to you therefore, brothers, by the mercies of God, to present your bodies as a living sacrifice, holy and acceptable to God, which is your spiritual worship.

It has been years in the making, but finally lawmakers and government agencies are jumping in to slow the progress of the opioid epidemic. It all started with the mass marketing and prescribing of painkilling drugs like oxycodone. Initially, the powers that be showed little concern for sufferers when crack cocaine was affecting people in the 1980s and 1990s. While we cradle those who unwittingly get addicted to prescription drugs, our solutions for crack addicts mostly consist of "locking them up" for as long as possible or letting them die. Truthfully, it appears that we are starting to do the right thing by heroin and opiate addicts, but a question still remains. Are we lifting the stigma for addiction, or is this a racial issue? Are we becoming more sympathetic or just showing our true feelings as a society about which lives matter the most?

In 1994, a bill passed that added more fuel to the fire. The sentence for crack possession and dealing was increased, and in a few years, enhanced law enforcement presence loomed over and aggressively policed black communities. So, our answer to drug addiction was this: intimidate, brutalize, and arrest. Compare that to now as pharmacies have begun to give addicts harm-reducing and abuse-deterring drugs. Narcan is now available over the counter, and overdoses can be reported to emergency dispatch with no fear of arrest. I can't even imagine that happening for crack addiction. In addition to the stigma that crack addiction has, there has traditionally been a huge sentencing disparity between two versions of the same drug. Crack cocaine possession carries three times the sentencing years as powdered cocaine. And it's the same drug—again, a reflection of our attitude toward blacks, or people of lower socioeconomic status.

Fortunately, the Fair Sentencing Act that passed in 2010 was supposed to take care of that, but I'm not sure how it's playing out. There are still some huge problems not addressed by the bill, such as reduced sentencing for persons prosecuted under the state law, which occurs the majority of the time. So where is the stigma coming from? Is it race, related to income level, or something to do with the substance itself?

While I suspect that race has a lot to do with it, I admit that, in the past, as a society we had little sympathy for addicts in any shape or form. Maybe this sudden outpouring of comparison and understanding means our views about addiction are finally changing. I just hope we continue and choose to consider all persons, regardless of color, social status, or substance of choice, as equally deserving of comparison and outreach.

The Rich Get Richer

A recent article written by Carmen Reinicke of CNBC is so sad that it is almost comical. According to Reinicke, the US income inequality is continuing to grow despite the rebound and growth of the economy. There is an ever-growing wage gap between the top 1 percent of wage earners and the bottom 99 percent. According to a 2015 survey, the top 1 percent of the American population makes 26.3 times what the bottom 99 percent makes. This is insane. How can it be that the average yearly income of the top 1 percent is 421,926 dollars per year, while the average yearly salary of the other 99 percent of the population is 50,107 dollars? And who are these 99 percent? Aren't they you and me? Aren't we the ones who actually *do* the work? Aren't we the workers who are going in early and coming home late? Aren't we the ones making our bosses rich? Then why must we lose sleep over how to keep the lights on, while the bosses have more money than they could ever spend? Corporate greed has reached an all-time high, or rather, an all-time low.

Between 1965 and 2016, the average median for family income has grown from 6,900 to 50,107 dollars annually. However, in that same time period, CEO pay has jumped from 20 times to 271 times that of a typical worker's salary.

So, in a nutshell, what we are seeing is an increase in economic growth but a lack of distribution of the wealth. The vast majority of the growth in the economy is being kept to further pad the pockets of those who are already rich, while the rest of the country is working hard and seeing little increase in wages.

Perhaps we can attribute this problem to the golden rule: the one with the gold makes the rules. Wealth is an influencer, and as we can see from this last election, money talks. A person with wealth can buy seats at the table that are unattainable to the other 99 percent of the country. And for this reason, there have been no regulations that hold water on how much of his profits a CEO must distribute to those who work for the company—thus the gross disparity in wages.

So now that we know this, what can we do to combat corporate greed? We need to consider making our side hustle our main vocation. We, as brothers, need to stop thinking that the "man" is going take care of us, because we have seen, on all fronts, that he will not. We need to stop being afraid to put our money together and build something of our own, where we are the CEO and decision maker. Yes, building a business is hard work, but if we are going to work hard anyway, shouldn't we be working to build a legacy for our children? Or better yet, the next time you walk into your place of business, think about who is really doing the work, and who will ultimately benefit from the sweat of your brow. Will it be you, or the top 1 percent?

The Wrong Perception

In 2016, Jason Goolsby decided to sue the District of Columbia for 1 million dollars in compensatory damages and 10 million in punitive damages. He and his friend were at an ATM waiting for the people in front of them to complete their transaction. While they were standing there, a woman phoned the police and informed them that she felt "uneasy" and uncomfortable with the two men outside at the ATM. She feared that she would be robbed. The police arrived at the scene within minutes and arrested Jason Goolsby and his friend Mike Brown. The two explained that they had done nothing wrong, and one of the teens began to film the incident on his cell phone. The confrontation escalated, and Jason Goolsby was thrown to the ground as he began to run from the police. His friend, Mike Brown, pushed a police officer and was also dragged to the ground. Later, the woman who had placed the call admitted that the two had done nothing to warrant arrest and that the police's actions had been excessive.

It probably will not take a rocket scientist to figure out that race played a major role in how this situation panned out. Jason Goolsby and his friend were black teens. The woman who made the call was white. The police who arrested them were white. And why were they arrested? Why was the call even validated? I call it the "Trayvon Martin effect." These two teens were not targeting anyone at that ATM; *they* were the targets. The white woman, being aware of her surroundings, had identified these two black teens as potential threats to her safety. If that was not bad enough, the police corroborated her bias by showing up and arresting Jason Goolsby and his friend.

No one deserves to be discriminated against and profiled. Perhaps the police pursued the teens in hopes of finding illegal guns or drugs that would then give them a reason to take the boys to jail. But after forcing them to the ground, they found nothing and released the boys without taking them into the station. Either way, it was racial profiling and unfair treatment based on bias. This is a story about perception and how the actions of certain people are often misconstrued. It is my hope that, one day, there is a precedent set that will change the way police officers respond to complaints that could be racially motivated.

The National Gentrification of the Inner City

Gentrification: the process of renovating and improving a house or district so that it conforms to middle-class taste. The term was coined by sociologist Ruth Glass.

"Once this process of 'gentrification' starts in a district it goes on rapidly until all or most of the original working-class occupiers are displaced and the whole social character of the district is changed."

—Ruth Glass (1964)

All over the United States, people are talking about what to do about public housing. While some see it as a hotbed for crime, unemployment, and abject poverty, others see it as an obligation of state and local governments to care for the elderly, handicapped, and disenfranchised. Perhaps nowhere in the country is the argument more prevalent than in the city of Atlanta, Georgia. Atlanta is a special case in the history of housing in the United States. It was the first city to develop public housing in 1936 and the first, early this century, to close it down completely in 2008, leaving all of its housing subject to the invisible hand of gentrification.

According to Jamiles Lartey of the *Guardian Magazine*, an analysis by the Governing magazine ranked Atlanta fifth among US cities experiencing the most gentrification, with more than 46 percent of its census tracts currently gentrifying. According to the city, median rents are up by 28 percent since 2000, compared with just 9 percent nationwide over the same time span. A 2018 report by HotPads found the rent in the city was rising three times faster than the national median. It also ranks third nationwide for evictions, with over four hundred cases being processed a month.

According to demographer William Frey of the Brookings Institution, the proportion of white people in Atlanta's population grew faster between 2000 and 2006 than in any other US city. While it is true that over the past twenty years there has been a steady flow of black Americans to the Atlanta region, they've mostly settled in suburbs to the north, leaving the city center itself disproportionately attracting white Americans. So, with rents getting higher, and tax assessments on the steady rise, where have the residents of the housing projects gone? And the better question is, does anyone care?

According to a 2009 article by Robbie Brown of the *New York Times*, the housing authority says that, in 2008, the overwhelming majority of residents supported the relocations. Thomas D. Boston, an economist at the Georgia Institute of Technology, said that those who move are more likely to find work, their children are likely to perform better in school, and they report higher satisfaction with their living conditions.

But critics say unsuspecting residents are forced into only marginally better neighborhoods. A large majority of displaced residents settle in ten of Atlanta's poorest ZIP codes, according to an analysis of housing authority data by *Creative Loafing*, an alternative newspaper. Only about 20 percent return to their communities once the property becomes a mixed-income development. "Until you have alternative housing that is affordable, available, and appropriate, you have no business going into these communities and destroying them," said Anita Beaty, the executive director of the Metro Atlanta Task Force for the Homeless. "To disperse these people without giving them alternatives is wrong."

The real winners, Ms. Beaty said, are business developers who make fortunes once the projects are torn down and the neighborhoods gentrify. For years, wealthier Atlantans, frustrated by long commutes, have been moving closer to their jobs downtown and displacing poorer residents to outlying suburbs. "Very much intertwined in all of this is the issue of race," said Deirdre Oakley, a professor of sociology at Georgia State University. "The people being affected are almost all poor African Americans."

Today, almost every major city in America, from Virginia to Chicago, has begun efforts to tear down public housing in favor of mixed income housing with government subsidy. The inner city is becoming more and more attractive to young professionals who prefer "work, live, play" environments where there is a minimal commute to work and easy access to the culture and night life of the city. As new housing replaces the projects and property taxes rise, more low-income tenants are forced to relocate under the burden of rising rents that will not be covered by their Section 8 voucher.

So, we see here that despite the fact that there is no answer to the question of what to do with the poor once gentrification has begun, it will continue until the city's original occupiers are completely displaced. And once again, the city's most vulnerable citizens are left to fend for themselves.

Makes Me Want to Holler

I just watched a movie called *Sorry to Bother You*, written and directed by Boots Riley. I'm not recommending it, but the movie brought up several big issues plaguing the black community such as incarceration, poverty, and racism. These issues were presented in the following ways:

- The movie depicted billboards in the black community advertising a "worry free lifestyle." These commercials and billboards showed entire families enjoying "three hot meals and a cot." The "worry free" facility starkly resembled a prison.

- The movie starred a young black man struggling to find employment to better himself. He receives employment at a telemarketing agency, only to find that he cannot sell the product unless he uses his "white voice," which he perfects, landing himself a promotion.

- The movie climaxes when the young man discovers that he and all of those in the "worry free lifestyle" are being turned into horse-like people who would be used to become the nation's free work force, thus reinstating slavery.

While this movie was a comedic satire, it shed light on real issues plaguing our nation in real time.

Why We Must Say Their Names

On July 22, 2018, three African American sisters—Nia, Letifah, and Tashiya Wilson—were attacked by a knife-wielding man, later identified as John Cowell, after exiting a Bay Area Rapid Transit (BART) train at MacArthur station in Oakland, California. Eighteen-year-old Nia Wilson died after her throat was slashed. Police brutality and hate crimes are public issues no one in this country really wants to talk about. When Nia Wilson was murdered, we were encouraged to "say her name" because, otherwise, no one would want to talk about it. The question is why. Why do we never want to talk about the issues that the police, those who are supposed to protect, and our fellow citizens, whom we are supposed to serve this nation alongside, inflict upon us? I hope to make it clear to you exactly why, regardless of whether or not we want to talk about it, we must.

The first reason why we, the African American community, must speak for ourselves is because if we don't, no one will. We must break the cycle of believing that as long as there is someone in the public spectrum who looks like us, we will be spoken for. Many will argue with me and say that this does not happen, but let us take a look at black America when Barak Obama was in office. Many believed that, since there was a black president, we would have to be advocated and spoken for. Barak Obama, however, was the president of all of the US citizens, which meant that he had to speak on behalf of the whole nation. This was not at all exclusive to colored people. Thus, many found themselves with not as much an advocate as they had hoped. While our community does have its own advocates, we cannot just depend on those in the public light to speak for us and expect that change will come about. We must stand up and speak for ourselves.

Another reason we must be our own spokesperson is to show that we will not be subdued. In the earlier days of this nation, it was not uncommon for a black person to be lynched, especially in the South. Lynchings happened when the white people of the area believed a black person did something wrong, disrespectful, or out of line. It was a method used by the white people of the day to keep people of color "in their place." Heinous as this act was, it worked for many years. Black people of that day constantly feared violence and thus lived in subordination to the white man—no longer a slave, but still in chains.

Today, we must still choose not to live in chains. We need to send a message that we will not be "put in our place." By choosing not to rise up and speak about the brutality that plagues our community, we choose to stay down and let our oppressors believe that they have indeed "put us in our place."

The third reason that we must never stay quiet is for the lives of those who have been killed. Nia Wilson was murdered. But before that, she had a life. She had a family and friends and people who loved her. She had hopes, dreams, aspirations, and plans for her future. She planned to join the army and become a paramedic. She was known for her kindness and motivation toward others. She was once seen performing the Heimlich maneuver on a stranger because he was choking. Nia Wilson was murdered for no reason. She never had a chance to join the army, become a paramedic, and make her parents and six siblings proud. That is why she must be spoken for. All of the people who have been hurt or killed as a result of police brutality and hate crimes had lives before they were taken. Their lives were important, and now that they can no longer speak for themselves, we must do it for them. Regardless of how we feel, we must say their names.

Kendrick Johnson

Kendrick Johnson was a high school student at Lowndes High School in Georgia. On January 11, 2013, his body was found wrapped in a gym mat in the school gymnasium. County sheriff's office ruled his death an accident. However, a private autopsy by Johnson's family ruled the cause of death as blunt force head trauma. In addition, Johnson's organs were never recovered from the coroner's office, so the family could not conduct further research as to their son's cause of death. There were also several cameras in the school that were missing the hours between the time Johnson walked into the gymnasium and his time of death. The family sued the board of education, stating that the school board, the police department, and the coroner's office were part of a conspiracy to cover up a homicide, aimed at protecting the killer, whose father was an FBI agent. Johnson's mother stated that she had visited the school to complain about the suspected killer, who had attacked Johnson more than once on school grounds because Johnson was having a relationship with his girlfriend. All of the county judges recused themselves from ruling on the case because of their relationship with the suspect's father. However, a ruling was made in a countersuit that ordered Johnson's family to pay more than 292,000 dollars in legal fees back to the county. To this day, no charges have been filed against the suspected killer, and Johnson's family is still fighting for justice for their son.

Racism and Classism Amid Natural Disaster: FEMA To Houston

In a repeat of the cruel politics of New Orleans, Houston, after being devastated in 2017 by hurricane Harvey, refused to pay on insurance policies for the poor and disenfranchised of the city, stating that they did not have flood insurance. This was a catch-22 for a community whose median income is 23,000 dollars a year. How can a family living below the poverty line afford extra insurance when they can barely afford to keep a roof over their head? They had nothing and no one to come to their aid to help them rebuild, except FEMA, who offered each family 4,300 dollars—enough to buy a bus or plane ticket to leave town. Maybe that is what the state wanted in the first place, because now those areas have new home signs and flags advertising two- and three-hundred-thousand-dollar homes to new homeowners.

Charlottesville and the Riot of Racism

Charlottesville, a quiet college town in Central Virginia, has for the second time in three years been on the national and global stage for racial conflict. In March 2015, Martese Johnson, a University of Virginia student leader, was beaten bloody outside of a bar near the university on St. Patrick's Day. His face was pounded by three officers for no apparent reason.

Know Better Do Better

At the onset, the officers claimed that Martese was drunk and was trying to enter the bar using a fake ID. Both allegations were later proven false. The incident, caught on many phone cameras, sparked days of protests about race relations in the city.

On August 12, 2017, more violence surrounding racial conflict broke out after various members of the Ku Klux Klan, neo-Nazis, and white nationalists met together to protest the removal of a confederate statue in the city. Here are the facts:

▪ A rally assembled on Saturday, August 12, to protest against the removal of a statue of confederate icon General Robert E. Lee.

▪ This rally was described as one of the largest white supremacist events in recent US history. It was organized by Jason Kessler, a former journalist and a member of the Proud Boys, an ultra-nationalist group. That Friday, marchers descended on the University of Virginia grounds carrying torches and yelling "white lives matter" and "blood and soil."

▪ Protesters gathered again on Saturday and clashed with counterdemonstrators.

▪ At 11:28 a.m., a local state of emergency was declared by

the City of Charlottesville

and the County of Albemarle.

▪ At 1:42 p.m., a racist protestor drove his car through a

group of anti-hate

demonstrators, killing thirty-two-year-old Heather Heyer

and injuring at least nineteen others.

▪ The speeding car fled the scene but was soon located and

stopped by police.

▪ James Alex Fields Jr. of Ohio was charged with second-

degree murder and other counts following the incident.

▪ A police force helicopter also crashed while in route to

the rally on Saturday, killing two state troopers.

On August 12, US President Donald Trump spoke of the

conflict as "violence on many sides." He refused to say that the

racist rally was wrong. He responded with a very general tweet

that read as follows: "We ALL must be united & condemn all

that hate stands for. There is no place for this kind of violence

in America. Let's come together as one!"

Two days later, after public outcry, he specifically

condemned white supremacy. But on Tuesday, he seemed to

angrily backtrack his comments, insisting that there was "blame on both sides," including anti-racist protesters. The remarks were welcomed by former Ku Klux Klan leader David Duke, who tweeted: "Thank you President Trump for your honesty & courage to tell the truth." So far, the aftermath of the Charlottesville incident has included candlelight vigils, fundraisers for the families of the deceased and injured, and anti-hate rallies across the country. The American Manufacturing Council and Strategy and Policy Forum ended after eight CEOs resigned over Trump's response to the Charlottesville violence. In North Carolina, a confederate flag was toppled. There still remains worldwide criticism of Donald Trump for his handling of the Charlottesville situation, with much blame and name calling from Donald Trump in his own defense.

The late Senator John Lewis, in a tearful speech, told listeners, "I cannot believe in my heart what I am witnessing today in America. I wanted to think not only as an elected official, but as a human being that we had made more progress. It troubles me a great deal."

Senator Bernie Sanders, in sharp contrast to Trump's statements, condemned the clashes and said, "(This) was a reprehensible display of racism and hatred."

A CBS News survey found the following:

• Fifty-five percent of the Americans polled said they disapproved of the president's response to the deadly violence.

• Sixty-seven percent of the Americans who approved were Republicans.

• Ten percent of the Americans who approved were Democrats.

• Americans are more likely to say Trump's policies have encouraged racial division (44 percent) rather than racial unity (12 percent).

Donald Trump's refusal to fully denounce both the racist attacks and his endorsements by the Klan speak volumes about the president's true feelings on racial equality. It is clear that black Americans do not have a friend in the White House.

Now that the lines have been drawn, what are we going to do? This is bigger than a confederate statue. This is about what kind of America we want ourselves and our children to live in. This is about whether or not we are going to allow this president and his followers to turn back the clock on race

relations in this country. Perhaps most importantly, this

situation should let us know that, unless we begin utilizing our

resources as citizens, we could very well lose them. We need to

pool our money to begin a full-scale media campaign against

racism and violence. We need to call our represented officials

and encourage them to raise their voices against racism and

violence. We need to support politicians and businesspeople

who have stood up to Trump and denounced his behavior

outright. KKK leader David Duke said that the weekend of

August 12 will be remembered as the day everything changed.

I agree that change is needed, but not in the way he desires. I

am calling on all Americans to make sure this change is a

positive one for all who call America home.

We must fight back against racism, but not with our fists.

We must fight with our money, our voice, and our vote.

Convenience Store Killings

On July 19 in Clearwater, Florida, Markeis McGlokton

was killed in front of his girlfriend and children. He had picked

up his girlfriend from her nursing shift and had stopped at a convenience store for snacks and drinks. She parked in a handicapped parking space and sent her boyfriend and five-year-old child into the store. While they were in the store, Michael Drejka, a white man, began yelling at her about the fact that she was parked in a handicapped spot despite being able-bodied. Upon seeing the altercation, Markeis intervened in her defense. He pushed Drejka down and proceeded to walk back into the store. At that point, Drejka pulled out a pistol and fired a single shot to the chest, killing McGlokton in front of his children and girlfriend. Initially, It was thought that Drejka would not be charged because he was standing his ground; however, Drejka was sentenced to twenty years in prison on October 11, 2019.

The threats to our rights and our freedoms are real. They are disheartening and beyond disturbing. As a parent, I fear for my children living in a world where black life is disregarded. At times, it seems that someone has written a memo to all the white people in the country saying, "Kill at will, and you'll get off." Truly the rash reality of two Americas—one for blacks, and one for everyone else—sometimes makes me want to holler and throw up my hands.

Lessons Learned from Hurricane Katrina

The city of New Orleans, Louisiana, has at least three major advantages: a fishing-based economy, oil wells that supply a large portion of the oil for this country, and a world-class tourist industry that is one of the largest in the country. However, New Orleans is also home to large communities of poor and underprivileged people. Crime and poverty are major concerns for citizens living there, and finally, much of the city sits below sea level.

Nobody expected Hurricane Katrina to be so severe. However, everybody knew that New Orleans was perhaps the most vulnerable city in America. It was already known that Katrina would hit Florida's coast first. But Florida's people had experience in storms and hurricanes. Long-time residents and some newcomers had the sense to listen to instructions from old-timers who knew what to do. They got what they needed—water, canned goods, boards, nails, and whatever they knew they would need—and took safe routes to safe areas. Although the storm in Florida was less severe, the trick was to listen to the report and decide if you were going to try to ride it out or leave. If you were going to leave, you had to get ready early or be trapped.

What happened in New Orleans was very different. FEMA wanted Mayor Ray Nagin to order the mandatory evacuation of New Orleans. But according to Nagin, the problem was a discrepancy in the information received by the mayor's and the governor's offices. The problem also lay in the unique economy of New Orleans.

In lower income areas, elderly residents of inner cities live quite differently than most of us. In certain areas, people live their entire lives in the inner city, and they go to school, work, and church without having a car or any other personal transportation. In their minds, a car is not a necessity, and if needed, the bus is always there.

An evacuation is far more frightening for someone whose life has been limited to an area such as the Lower Ninth Ward. It's hard for people to leave the homes they have lived in all their lives. Are they expected to pack up with their families, clothes, food, and blankets and leave without a car? Please understand that the mayor had to take all of this into consideration before he ordered a full coast evacuation.

If Nagin had chosen to evacuate the city and the storm had hit as it did, he would have been a hero, and FEMA would have been coordinating the care, feeding, and ultimate recovery of the people who had been evacuated. However, if the storm had veered off into the sea, as had happened in the past, those evacuated would have had their lives disrupted for no reason. The mayor would have then had to bear the burden of seeing his city struggle financially from the cost of needless evacuation. They could have had to face possible lawsuits from area businesses and citizens alike. He would also have likely lost in the next election—catch-22.

While this is true, Ray Nagin's judgment call not to order a mandatory evacuation failed, because he was wrong on three points. Strike one was that he thought the hurricane would go out to sea. Strike two was that he thought the hurricane would reduce itself to a storm. Strike three was that he thought the levees would hold. So now he's out.

But Nagin was not the only guilty party in all of this. We need to get something straight. Many people believe that FEMA or the Department of Homeland Security somehow have an army of people ready to engage at a moment's notice if a natural disaster should occur. Not so.

Louisiana's National Guard was working at about half its usual strength in August 2005. Four thousand men and women were available for service. The other half, however, had been called to duty in Iraq.

Secondly, the states have the first responsibility to respond to a crisis and assess needs that exceed their available resources. Only when the response, recovery, and disaster team is able to assess the situation, and find that the burden is too much for the state, will FEMA respond. Ray Nagin's failure to order a timely mandatory evacuation meant that all other timelines were affected as well.

And here comes the part where you come in. The American people are not guiltless in the devastating outcomes of Hurricane Katrina. The more visual part of the story of the survivors was playing out on live TV from the Superdome. The corpses rotting and stinking in the streets, with few people available to remove them, proved to be a great visual for the news. Everyone saw the images, including the NAACP, members of the Congressional Black Caucus and all of the decision makers in Washington. If all of this were not enough to get us moving, what would it take?

Now I know there were people, heroes really, who stayed in New Orleans and worked as hard as they could. In the weeks following the storm, Carnival cruise line sent three cruise ships. A cruise ship is a floating city that thousands of people can be housed in. An airline put up some of their planes to fly people where they wanted to go. The Navy sent a hospital ship with fifteen operating rooms; however, Senator Lott of Mississippi had it rerouted to Mississippi instead.

To this date, all of these supports have returned to normal business and the problem of reconstruction remains unsolved. I believe the public should have helped more. Even now, help is still needed in New Orleans.

In all the images we saw over the Internet, the focus was almost always on the poor racial minorities and the limited availability of resources in that frightening position. As citizens sat on top of their roofs begging to be rescued, ugly rumors spread that the people were shooting at their rescuers. In reality, they were simply attempting to attract the attention of the helicopters. Did we use those rumors as an excuse not to send more help? Or do we think that poor people are somehow less deserving of the country's efforts?

We live in a nation of surplus. So, bringing in supplies may have been delayed, but it should not have been long enough to be a pervasive problem. Did we allow the initial delays to be our excuse to not send money and supplies? Even many people of New Orleans who had been only mildly affected, instead of helping the less fortunate, concentrated their attention on protecting their own property with shot guns. What a sad commentary on the value of human life.

At the Superdome, there were thirty thousand people waiting for transportation, and there were another twenty-five thousand people in the convention center waiting for evacuation and transportation to anywhere. These people needed our help, and as a nation, we failed them.

Let me also note that the city of New Orleans had some unique issues of its own. Many of the people living in the Ninth Ward had lived and played around the levee all their lives. Some lived at a stone's throw from the levee. Living in the Ninth Ward next to the levee was a part of life. People ignored the fact that the levees were only built to withstand the force of the most frequent hurricanes: Category 3. New Orleans didn't normally get hurricanes of 4 and 5. So why worry about it? For many of those living in New Orleans, all the warning was about something that may or may not happen. The levees looked strong and impenetrable and may have given the residents a feeling of false security. California, for example, gets earthquakes all the time. But the people there, who can afford to live any place in the world, choose to live where they know there is a chance of a big earthquake happening at any time. They believe it will not happen, at least not in their lifetime. That was probably the same attitude the people of New Orleans had. It was no secret that the levees were old and in need of repair. But nothing had ever happened to them, and so no one was worried.

Earthquakes, floods, hurricanes, and volcano eruptions are real possibilities in some of the most populous states in the country. And the fact is that we have no control over these things, and we should take that into consideration. We need to find a way to prepare for any event that might happen.

The severity of this storm also left New Orleans with severe budget problems. City bus drivers and other critical personnel, law enforcement officers, emergency medical personnel, and a host of other city employees were put on overtime just after the storm. Those who stayed worked tirelessly to try and make a positive impact where they could. Money was spent for special equipment such as water rescue vehicles, and the budget suffered. There was just not enough state money to help the enormous number of people who suddenly had nothing.

We must realize that the tipping point for the catastrophe was the element of surprise. Then there was the issue of the timeline. Then Mayor Nagin made the wrong call. Then FEMA was not organizationally prepared to handle this type of disaster. Then there was a delay in getting qualified people to the critical areas. And on top of that, the people were assured that the levees were built to withstand strong winds. But on August 27, 2005, by 5:00 a.m., Hurricane Katrina came through New Orleans with winds at 115 miles per hour. The levees gave way, parts of the city went underwater, and most of

Know Better Do Better

America, including its president, looked on and did nothing to help. Shame on you. Shame on me. Shame on us all.

Who Owns What?

On March 30, 2014, columnist John Olen published an article in Economy in Crisis listing the number of American corporations that are now owned by foreign companies. As of today, the list continues to grow. As a matter of fact, if you went to the movies this weekend, you probably didn't know that, when you paid for your ticket at an AMC theater, you paid it to a company owned by the Chinese. It is estimated that by 2033, a whopping 51 percent of all-American businesses will be under foreign control. We see this happening right under our noses. Who would have thought that Samsung would ever outsell Sony in this country? This company is now going after Apple. Household names like Adidas, Church's chicken, Caribou Coffee, and Virginia's own Smithfield Hams have recently been sold to foreign entities while continuing to sell their product in American venues. The following list is far from exhaustive and continues to grow daily.

Budweiser, now owned by Anheuser-Busch InBev NV, which is based in Leuven, Belgium

Alka-Seltzer, now owned by German company Bayer Schering Pharma AG

Ben & Jerrys, now owned by British-Dutch Unilever

AMC theaters, now owned by the Chinese

7-Eleven, now owned by the Japanese company Seven & I Holdings

Woman's Day Magazine, now owned by the French company Hachette Filipacchi Médias, S.A.

Purina, now owned by the Swiss company Nestle

Gerber, now owned by the Swiss pharmaceutical giant Novartis

Firestone, now owned by the Japanese Bridgestone Corporation

Citgo, now owned by the government of Venezuela

French's Mustard, now owned by Reckitt Benckiser, a British conglomerate

Frigidaire, now owned by Sweden's AB Electrolux

The Plaza Hotel in New York City, now owned by Israeli billionaire Yitzhak Tshuva's El-Ad Group

Know Better Do Better

Trader Joes, now owned by German billionaires Karl and Theo
Albrecht

Dial soap, now owned by Henkel, KGaA, based in Dusseldorf,
Germany

Sunglass Hut, now owned by Italian eyewear seller Luxottica
Group

I don't believe anyone should dispute the right of any person or country to own businesses or property; however, I do believe that doing better means that everyone seeks to take hold of the opportunities before them, whether it be home ownership, land ownership, or business ownership. With the ownership of property and businesses comes the ability to elevate your financial place in your community.

At the time of writing this book, Canadian Pacific remains focused on merging with Norfolk Southern, one of the biggest railroad companies in the country. My problem is this: If immigrant communities and foreign enterprises can buy out this country, why can't the African American community buy a company? Statistically speaking, black people collectively make more than enough money to be a driving force in this country. We just need to put our money together. We need to get to the bottom of why this is hard for the African American community when other minority groups do it all the time. Do we not trust our fellow African Americans? We can talk about this thing forever, but when it is time to put our money where our mouths are, it is always a different story. I do not believe it is in our DNA, as Trump would suggest. This is a lingering product of slavery that I believe we can fight against and overcome. There was a time when we only had to worry about other Americans getting ahead of us in wealth. Now we have to contend with the fact that people from everywhere have begun to make investments in this country and have surpassed us in attaining a portion of our country's wealth. The pie is only so big, and our time is limited.

Black Wealth in Numbers

Ok, black community, I've got some good news and some bad news, and some more good news. I will give the good news first. Congratulations! Black wealth is rising! African American spending power has surpassed 1.3 trillion dollars annually! Something to shout about, right? Wrong.

Know Better Do Better

Here is the bad news. We are spending our money in ways that are keeping us in socioeconomic poverty and leaving our children with nothing to build on after we are gone. We have the tools to raise our political, social, and financial status as a race, yet we have not put our hands to the work. Let's explore this further.

The following statistics are taken from the study "Resilient, Receptive and Relevant: The African-American Consumer 2013 Report," a collaborative effort by the Nielsen Company in New York and the National Newspaper Publishers Association (NNPA), located in Northwest Washington, DC.

- Black buying power continues to increase, rising from its current 1.1-trillion-dollar level to a forecasted 1.3 trillion dollars by 2017.

- Despite the strong economic outlook, blacks continue to spend most of their money outside of the black community.

- Each year, blacks spend more than 47 billion dollars on Lincoln automobiles, 3.7 billion dollars on alcohol, 2.5 billion dollars on Toyotas, 2 billion dollars on athletic shoes, and 600 million dollars each year on McDonald's and other fast foods, according to Target Market News Inc., a Chicago-based marketing research group.

- Blacks also spend wildly to keep up their appearances. The black hair care and cosmetics industry counts as a 9-billion-dollar-a-year business, but while African Americans are spending the most, they are profiting the least, said officials from the Black Owned Beauty Supply Association (BOBSA) in Palo Alto, California. Beauty product lines designed for African Americans were once 100 percent owned and operated by blacks. Today, other ethnic groups control more than 70 percent of the market.

According to the State of Working America, black people spend 4 percent more money annually than any other race despite the fact that they are the least represented race and the race that lives in poverty at the highest rate.

If current economic trends continue, the average black household will need 228 years to accumulate as much wealth as their white counterparts hold today. For the average Latino family, it will take 84 years (Institute for Policy Studies, IPS,

and the Corporation for Economic Development).

Here are the facts. Our spending has got to change. We

are acting like children with our "new" money, preferring to

spend on cars, shoes, and other expensive food—things that

bring instant gratification and no long-term stability—than to

spend on things that will uplift our families in the long run.

You have seen what we spend on. Now look at what we are not

spending our money on.

Whites have more saved for retirement than blacks and Hispanics

$130,472 — Whites

$19,049 — Blacks

$12,329 — Hispanics

A dollar circulates

- six hours in the black community (about the time it takes for

    your check to clear at midnight, and for you to make

    your coffee stop the next morning),

- seventeen days in the white community,

- twenty days in the Jewish community, and

- thirty days in the Asian community.

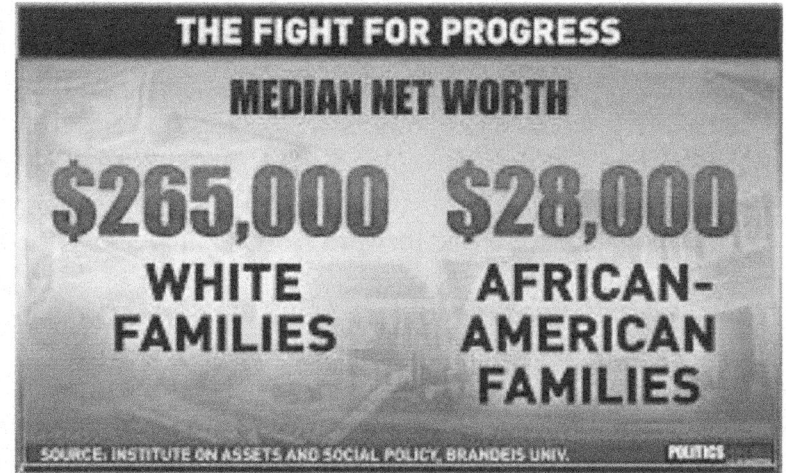

- So, once again, here are the facts. We are spending

sufficiently, but not on the things that build wealth. We are not

saving for retirement, nor spending money in black-owned

businesses or banks. Therefore, we are contributing to the

building of white and Asian wealth and depleting our

communities of the resources it needs to build our own wealth.

This is why African Americans lag so miserably behind in net

wealth. We are digging our own graves with our own golden

shovels! Yes, the hand we were dealt was a poor one. Yes,

America has not treated us equally. Yes, we have been

oppressed. But right here and right now, we cannot blame the white man for our personal spending habits any more than Eve could rightly blame the serpent for tempting her to sin. The white man is not doing this to us. We are doing this to ourselves. We are the only ones who can help us. Nobody else is going to.

So, how can we move forward from what we now know to be the truth? It all starts with the man in the mirror. You and those who you talk to and interact with can start along a better path. It will not happen overnight, but change is possible. www.letsbuyblack365.com is an excellent resource where you can type in any type of business you are looking for and get connected to a black-owned business in your area. A small step toward buying smarter can make a big difference in our community. Let's call on black entertainers, athletes, and musicians to stop negatively influencing the community by throwing away money in clubs and start some real dialogue on how to use money as a tool to build real wealth. We can assess our spending by making larger pretax contributions to our 401K and finding ways to invest pretax dollars in other savings mechanisms to ensure that we can have money to send our kids to college, or at least not force our children to throw a bake sale to bury us. Most employers have financial strategists available to employees free of charge. We just need to make the appointment.

Also, we can avoid these five pitfalls, written by blogger Matthew Corbin who wrote "5 Reasons Why Black People Are Still Broke":

1. Black people spend more money than they make.

2. Black people don't support black businesses.

3. Black people don't save their money.

4. Black people don't know how to invest.

5. Black people aren't working towards getting out of poverty. The following is an excerpt from an article entitled "How Black Dollars Can achieve Black Power" by author William Reed.

"Opportunities exist across the nation for black individuals, their organizations, churches, lodges, frats and entrepreneurs to provide educational programs, workshops and business conferences that teach and show people how and why to do for self. America needs local black leadership demonstrating the power of the black dollar and increase community awareness to recycle dollars within our community, by banking with black-owned banks and buying from black businesses. The solution to the high unemployment and income inequality [in] black communities must come from us. It includes development of black businesses. Local or national groups, be them small or large: the thing is to do for self. If we are serious about tackling unemployment in our community, the quickest fix is to start financially supporting black-owned businesses. Too many blacks rely on getting whites to remedy their financial problems. Data suggests that if African Americans invested more money in black-owned businesses, these businesses would be sources of employment for more of us.

The stand we suggest all blacks adopt is empowering the black community toward taking control and redirecting its wealth and investments. Blacks need more education on consuming and capitalism. More blacks must establish locations where people come and learn economic and financial principles on how to create and sustain black businesses where they live. Let's more of us hold more power networking conferences for training and networking to bolster and educate blacks. We all have to engage what we know and have toward operational unity. Enterprising individuals and organizations can sponsor regular business networking socials and gatherings. Do them at black-owned establishments. Be sure to invite blacks in banking. Those provide opportunities for entrepreneurial blacks to meet one another, exchange ideas and partner."

So, in closing, much has been said on this issue, but there is still so much more to say. We can baby step our way to a whole new life if we are willing to put forth the work. Not an all at once type of short-lived change, but a number of small consistent changes can produce larger long-term results. The scriptures tell us that this race is not given to the swift nor to the strong, but to the one who endures to the end. We have to keep teaching on financial freedom. We need to keep saying it, and saying it, and saying it, until it becomes more of a heart truth than a head truth. This will take time, but it can be done, one person, family, and community at a time. Who will be the one to be the change we all want to see in the black community?

Lies Black People Believe about Race and the Truth that Sets Them Free

According to the documentary *7AM* by Black Film & Media, every problem that black people have is directly related to a lack of money. Consider the following examples:

- African Americans are the poorest people in the United States.

- There is no path to wealth for the employee, only the employer.

- When the Civil War ended in 1865, African Americans controlled about one half of 1 percent of the nation's wealth. Today, in 2015, African Americans still own only about one half of 1 percent of the wealth worldwide. Here in the United States, African Americans won about one-third of 1 percent of the wealth worldwide.

- All other ethnic groups have various levels of an inheritance cycle. Black people often only pass on poverty.

- Twenty-four percent of African Americans have no assets other than a car.

- African Americans are the biggest consumers. We buy everything and own nothing.

- Business is largely controlled along ethnic lines. When a person of a particular ethnic group starts a business, the trend is to employ family members, friends, and others of their own ethnicity.

- Racism is the removal of wealth and resources from the hands of black folks.

- Politics decides who gets the benefits in life. It is all about quid pro quo. One hand washes the other. Once elected, politicians do for those who put them in office. Black elected officials have largely been silent on race issues affecting their jurisdictions because of the origins of the money and power that put them in office.

- Million-dollar sports players often have income but not wealth because the income is controlled by the owners. Injuries could take them from a mansion to the project within a few years.

- Wealth means that you own it, control it, and can pass it down.

- Marcus Garvey stated that the issue keeping us from coming together to pool resources is that we are a people plagued by petty differences.

In the end, we need to love each other and trust each other enough to take some of our money back from handbags, cars, and vacations, and put it in a pot with other blacks to build an airline, or invent something, or run our own sports team, or build homes to keep our communities strong.

Poverty and the Food Desert

Karla and Jermaine Scott go to the grocery store once a month. When they go, they plan to be out for three hours. The grocery store is twelve miles from their home. It takes about two transfers and a fifteen-minute walk in both directions from the bus stop to the front door of their apartment. Between trips to the grocery store, they must rely on the Little Giant, a local convenience store that sells hot dogs, French fries, fried chicken, milk, eggs, cigarettes, and alcohol. They will pay two-thirds more for milk and eggs than they would at the grocery store further away in an upscale neighborhood. Karla and James, along with twenty-five to thirty million other low-income Americans, live in food desert.

A food desert is an area where there is more access to fast food and junk food than to healthy food choices. In low-income areas throughout the country, the nearest grocery store is located miles away. This creates problems for those who do not have access to personal transportation. However, the chips become stacked against residents of low-income neighborhoods when fast food advertising is fifteen times greater in these areas than in middle- and upper-class neighborhoods. Nationwide, 72 percent of restaurants in low-income areas are fast food restaurants, compared to only 41 percent in middle- and upper-class neighborhoods. Furthermore, low-income neighborhoods on average have more stores that sell alcohol and cigarettes.

Perhaps the most shameful fact is that residents of the food deserts are paying more for their food than those who live in middle- and upper-class neighborhoods. Those who live on or below the poverty line are being further penalized by low access to healthy food that is competitively priced and are given disproportionate access to fast food that is not only devoid of nutrition but is more expensive.

Residents of our poorest neighborhoods have the least access to healthy foods, the highest rate of fast food advertising, the highest rate of alcohol and tobacco advertising, a 30 percent markup on household grocery items, and an increased risk of death by health-related illness. Is this a coincidence?

Further Benefits to the Wealthy through Outsourcing

Tata Consulting Services in Mumbai has received many visas in the past five years. The federal government passed a law allowing American companies to grant visas to foreign workers. The stipulation was that those hired from outside of the country would possess specialized skills and work on a temporary basis to meet the needs of the companies. However, to date, Tata Consulting has issued several visas to workers from India, mostly in the areas of accounting and back-office administration. Meanwhile, these same companies are laying off American employees. It is speculated that, ultimately, these employers are seeking to take these jobs to India to avoid paying American salaries. They are also requiring that the American workers train their foreign replacements before layoff so as to cause no decline in productivity. This appears to be a decline in morality and an increase in corporate greed.

This is just one example of government policies that only benefit the rich and leave the common man to pick up the pieces. This outsourcing is happening in companies such as Toys R Us, New York Life, and Disney World. These are the same companies that made their fortunes from the same American workers that are now being laid off. In 2007, after the stock market crash, it was companies such as these that went to the federal government asking for a bailout. While I cannot ascribe to an American-only or American-first philosophy, it does seem that American companies should prioritize American workers.

Another American corporation problem lies in the gap between the CEO and the worker wage getting wider. In 2015, the secretaries and exchange made it official. Public companies will soon have to say exactly how much their chief executive's pay compares with the typical employee. At America's biggest companies, the top boss makes more than 300,000 dollars for every 100 dollars earned by its typical employee. This is up from a 20 to 1 ratio in 1965. For example, if a worker makes 10 dollars an hour, their CEO could make as much as 300 dollars per hour. If the worker is making 15 dollars an hour, the CEO would then make 450 dollars per hour. The board of the company determines most CEO salaries. While this may seem democratic, the CEO appoints most members of the board. Furthermore, many board members have been found to be longtime business partners, friends, CEOs of partnering companies, and even family members of the CEO. One thing is certain. These board members have an interest in seeing the CEO get what he wants. As this gap continues to increase, so does the gap between the richest and the poorest in America. This steady widening income disparity raises the question of who is looking out for the interests of the workers who labor in these companies year after year. The company as a whole should be working for the best interest of its workforce because, without them, the company could not prosper. Or does the CEO do all of the work? When will the worker and the people on the front line get their piece of the pie?

Learning and Moving Forward from Tragedy

Ferguson

After the killing of an unarmed teenager named Michael Brown in the summer of 2014 in Ferguson, Missouri, at the hand of a white police officer, the black community took to the streets with slogans, rallies, and marches to protest this and other acts of unprovoked violence at the hands of police officers. The protests lasted over two weeks and received national and international coverage and debate. The attorney general at the time, Eric Holder, upon visiting the city, launched a federal investigation into this city's judicial branch. The findings, although not surprising, revealed the atrocious racial bias practiced on a regular basis by the police forces and courts system in Ferguson.

The March 4, 2015, edition of the *Virginian-Pilot* reported these facts regarding the justice department's findings of rampant racism in the Ferguson Police Department. Although blacks make up 67 percent of the population, they accounted for 93 percent of arrests between 2012 and 2014. The officials also found that black motorists from 2012 to 2014 were more than twice as likely as whites to be searched during traffic stops even though they were 26 percent less likely to be found at fault, and that blacks were 68 percent less likely than others to have their cases dismissed by a municipal court judge. From April to September of last year, 95 percent of people kept at the city jail for more than two days were black. Of the cases in which the police department documented the use of force, 88 percent involved blacks, and of the fourteen dog bite victims, all were black. The report details a criminal justice system that issues citations for petty infractions such as walking in the middle of the street, putting the raising of revenue from fines ahead of public safety. This practice hits poor people especially hard, sometimes leading to jail time when they cannot pay. The tussle that led to Michael Brown's death began after former officer Wilson told him and a friend to move from the street to the sidewalk. Among the report's findings were racially tinged emails stating that President Obama would not be president for very long because what black man holds a steady job for four years. Another described black women having abortions as a way to curb crime.

"The murder of Michael Brown was part of a systemic pattern of inappropriate policing of African American citizens in the Ferguson community," said, Benjamin Crump, the attorney for the Brown family. In essence, this statement along with the Department of Justice findings suggest that bias exists within the police department as a whole, as well as in the court system.

This battle can only be conquered from the inside out. Darren Wilson resigned from the Ferguson police force after being cleared of wrongdoing in the killing of unarmed teen Michael Brown. On March 18, 2015, Ferguson City manager John Shaw resigned in light of the justice department's reports. Yet these two men were only pieces of a bigger puzzle of bigotry where it is considered a procedure to single out blacks without cause. That was then and now is the time for the black community of Ferguson to have a voice and a presence in the operations of this city.

According to an August 8, 2014, article by Ian Mikhisen of thinkingprocess.com, only 6 percent of eligible voters cast a ballot in the Ferguson municipal elections. This is compared to 55 percent of black voters who turned out in the

2012 presidential elections. While it is important to have their voices heard at the White House, it is of equal or greater importance for the welfare of blacks in Ferguson and other minority cities.

Blacks have marched and waved signs and worn the t-shirts. Now it is time for qualified individuals to be courageous enough to be the change that is needed in court systems and police forces in Ferguson and so many other cities across this nation. Without a black presence on the police forces and in the courts, these systems will continue to be allowed to operate in a corrupt and unconstitutional manner that targets and convicts a race of people before they ever commit a crime. As long as the black community refuses to take an active role in our city, state, and federal legislature, the problem will continue to exist. Deuteronomy 3:18: *The Lord himself will lead you and be with you. He will not fail you or abandon you, so do not lose courage or be afraid.*

Could Somebody Please Tell Me What is Going On, When Our Country Refuses to Look for Missing African Americans?

Teens are going missing by the dozens in our nation's capital, and no one seems concerned. Thirty-four teenagers, all black and Latino, some as young as twelve years old, were reported missing in the district in the month of March 2017. Out of the thirty-four reported missing, eleven have still not been found.

To date, over five hundred young people have been reported missing in the district in the first three months of 2017.

Chanel Dickerson, commander of Washington, DC, police department's youth services division, says that she took to social media to alert the world about the missing girls in order to quickly bring resolution and awareness to the problem. She states that the number of missing teens in the district has actually decreased over the years and that the majority of the thirty-four teens missing have either left home voluntarily or have been reunited with their families. The district police department says that the cases are unrelated and that there is no reason to believe that the missing youths have been abducted for sex trafficking. She says that the numbers are not out of the normal range of missing persons cases, and that the nation should not be alarmed.

Everybody is saying to calm down, but I can't keep calm. There are too many questions that still remain. Are we saying that these staggering numbers of missing teens is a common occurrence? Or are we pushing much bigger child welfare issues under the rug? In a January 17 issue of the *Washington Post*, Colbert King wrote, "Right here in the nation's capital, our most vulnerable residents — children — are subjected to sex slavery. Their stories don't make the evening news or even warrant blurbs in your morning paper. But human trafficking is, and has been, a shadowy and seamy part of D.C. life."

Do we know what happens to these teens while they are out of custodial care? If not, how can we rule out the sex trafficking ring that is thriving in our nation's capital and across the country? When abducted children are found, what then? Is there a manhunt for the abductor, or is the case simply closed and taken off the books? Julia Craven of the *Huffington Post* writes, "The Black and Missing Foundation, founded in

2008, is one of few organizations that aims to bring awareness to missing people of color." Derrica Wilson, co-founder and chief executive of the organization, says 40 percent of missing persons in the United States are people of color.

Most of them are black or Latino. "How often do you see an Amber alert for a missing black or brown kid?" Wilson said. "They like to classify our kids as runaways [and] runaways do not get the Amber Alert."

Perhaps the biggest question I have is why the majority of the teens missing in this particular case were African American when the black population in Washington, DC, is only 50 percent. If the cases are unrelated, why do these unsung tragedies only seem to hit our communities? And why have we heard so little about these cases? Where are the nationwide manhunts for these teens? Where is the around-the-clock news coverage? Where are the social media hashtags? Where are their Amber alerts? Why are these kids labeled as runaways without adequate proof? Where is the legislation passed to honor their lives? Why aren't their pictures on the covers of national newspapers? Where are their stories on the grocery store magazine racks? Where are the high-profile interviews and press conferences with their parents? Why are these teens being forgotten? Who is looking for them? And why does this sting feel so familiar? Perhaps because this is just another case where America tells black people that our lives just don't matter.

Chapter Two

Thoughts on the Poor of Our Communities

Focus on the Family produced a study on Biblical world view called "The Truth Project." In this study, the speaker seeks to reveal Biblical truths in every facet of life and to help the learners separate themselves from the lies that are prevalent in the world. These life topics include God, man, ethics, history, authority, significance, religion, morality, work, economics, and culture. In the final video of the series, the speaker talks about economy, money, and our responsibilities toward God concerning wealth. We as Christians might all agree that money should be used as a tool and should not be worshipped. We would probably all agree that man should work to support his family. We would perhaps all agree that we should help the poor and ill of our communities. However, the big clash would be about how we should help the poor. Our churches as well as our political parties are divided on this subject. According to the Truth Project, there are a few Biblical examples that tell us how God wants us to relate to the poor. In Ruth 2:2, when Ruth and her mother-in-law return to their hometown poor and without any male to provide for them, "Ruth the Moabitess said unto Naomi, 'Let me now go to the field, and glean ears of corn after him in whose sight I shall find grace.'"

According to this series, the process of gleaning is a Biblical act that shows us how God wants those who "have" to treat those who "do not have," and sets a precedent for what we should do today as believers.

- Gleaning requires thoughtfulness and generosity on the part of the landowner. The owner was required to only take the first scraping of the crops and to not repeat the process to get all of the harvest. What was left over after the first harvesting was left for the poor to come and pick up so that they would not starve.

- Gleaning requires willingness on the part of the gleaner. Ruth worked from morning until evening and came each day to the field to get corn to provide for herself and her mother-in-law.

- The gleaning process created a posture of favor. The landowners knew how blessed they were, the gleaners were blessed from what was left over, and the supply came from God.

- This gleaning situation also created opportunities for the landowner to bless those gleaners in whom he found special favor. In Ruth 2:16 the landowner says to his harvesters about Ruth, "And let fall also some of the handfuls on purpose for her and leave them that she may glean them." This process allowed those looking for work to present themselves as hard-working and dependable so that they may be considered for a more permanent position.

According to the Truth Project series, the modern-day methods by which the poor are provided for rob both wealthy and poor of these types of opportunities to bless and be a blessing.

Our welfare system is set up to provide for the poor and disabled. If you qualify under certain conditions, you can receive housing allowances, food stamps, and money every month. However, under these conditions, you can rarely have two working adults in the home, go to school to better yourself, or get a promotion on your job, because that could easily disqualify you from these benefits. Over the years, a culture has been created that no longer strives to care more for than

taken care of the poor. It also causes the working class to have

a disdain and arrogance concerning welfare recipients and the

poor in general, considering them an underclass of lazy people.

Many people panhandle on the streets of our cities, with

signs to promote pity and generosity. We as Christians are torn

on these issues because we are aware that shelters and

treatment programs exist that could help many. We wonder

whether we are being scammed and taken advantage of, and

often look the other way when we don't want to think about the

destitute of our own communities.

But could there be a better way? Should those who

panhandle actually be asking for work? And should we as land

and business owners be looking for the poor and give them

jobs where they might be able to earn money and rebuild their

lives? Perhaps. There are four main factors that the current

welfare system has not addressed.

1. Value of work: Many welfare recipients are

   robbed of the value of work and are therefore

   unable to teach this value to their children. If the

system is going to take care of them, why should they strive to get good grades in school, go to college, or enter the workforce? There must be a way to provide for our poor without robbing them of the value of work.

2. Self-value: Men and women alike place value on themselves based on their ability to produce. Getting a reward without working for it lowers the esteem of the person and the process. As a result, people have less regard for themselves and others and less regard for work as a means to wealth and success. This may account for higher rates of crime in areas that are poor or densely populated by welfare recipients.

3. Drive in other areas of life: Earning a living and being an asset to society is ingrained in our DNA, no matter how hard we try to fight it. God designed man to work and take pride in what he does. If the opportunity for an able-bodied person to earn his/her rightful place in society is taken away, it is quite possible that there will be

a lack of drive in other areas of that person's life. We see that in a generational repeat of families—mothers, daughters, and grandchildren—who are all trapped in the welfare system, with little hope (or desire) to get out.

4. Lastly, giving funds instead of earning funds robs both the giver and the receiver in the relationship. Those in the position to give complain of having to spend their tax dollars on people who don't want to work. Those in the position to receive complain that they can't get anywhere in life because the system is keeping them down. However, if those who needed work were actually seeking it from both corporations and private citizens, and those who needed jobs done were looking to the forgotten work pool of the poor, perhaps more unemployed people would have jobs. Perhaps there would also be greater opportunity for those who are willing to

work to find favor in the eyes of those who have
work to give.

The story of Ruth began with her willingness to work hard to provide food for her family. While there, she found favor in the eyes of a landowner named Boaz who admired her hard-working spirit and gave her favor and protection in the fields. As time went on, a relationship began, and eventually Boaz agreed to absorb all of Ruth's debt by becoming her kinsman redeemer. Perhaps the story in the black community could be similar. Those who are poor in our community are given jobs by those who are in position to provide employment. This would mean that those who are able to become business owners should do so in an effort to promote from within. Eventually certain workers find favor in the eyes of their employers and form relationships. Finally, skills are passed on that allow the poor to provide for themselves and better their station in life. Could this happen in our generation? I believe so.

If We Want to be Successful, We Need Money Sense and We need to Unite

We live in a capitalist system. Here, the rules are simple. Learn them and move up, or else. If you are not pursuing the American dream, then what are you pursuing? I'll let you in on a secret. If you are not seeking to get your finances under control, poverty will pursue you. You will need to work hard, and no one is going to give you a medal for it. You will need to save your money to put toward personal and family goals. Even though the commercials tell us to spend, spend, spend, we will need to think twice about how we are using our hard-earned dollars.

People will tell you to avoid the temptation of getting money and keeping it in savings accounts. They say things like, "Tomorrow is not promised." "Just be happy and everything will be alright." I listen to people talk about the evils of wealth. But these people sound like new fools to me. You don't have to be a money hoarder, but everyone should care about how they use the money God gives them. We should care about working hard, because it is what we are supposed to do, and it is the only way to create a better life for ourselves and our families.

This is not a socialist system, and no one is going to give us anything. Everything costs. So, we have got to live and work in the system we have and come up with ways to make it work for us. Here are just a few rules that have been instrumental for me.

- Don't seek to be the norm; seek to be the exception in your family, community, and your world.

- The mess always flows down to the bottom. So, we should not be at the bottom. Never stop strategizing to rise above.

- The black community must unify in our thinking. We should all want to see our brothers and sisters prosper, because it makes the pursuits of those coming behind us easier.

- There will always be the temptation to take the path of least resistance. So, recognize it, fight against it, and tell others to do the same.

- Always speak up for the poor working-class men and women in this country. People who go to work every day and work hard should be able to bring home a wage that allows them to feed their children.

I don't know how a person can keep a straight face and say that we don't need to raise minimum wage. Some people just don't understand that a loaf of bread, a gallon of milk, and a gallon of gas costs the working poor man the same amount that it costs the rich man. They both need these items, but for the poor working man, it takes more stress, more hardship, and more sacrifice to do so.

- Be a foot soldier against poverty, racism, and all systems that exploit the poor in the name of the almighty dollar.

- Never look down on a person for working harder and longer to make a better life for themselves. Always encourage those who are trying.

- Once you get the "better life" you were seeking, reach back to try to help and teach others how to do the same.

Self-Inflicted Wounds (Some of This is Our Own Fault)

Suicide Mentality

Since 1985, obesity rates for all Americans have increased, including those for teens and very young children. African Americans are currently leading the pack, with over 48 percent of all African American adults being overweight. As of 2015, obesity rates for African American women has continued to increase, making black women twice as likely to be extremely overweight as white women. Currently, the obesity rate for black women in America is at a staggering 57.2 percent. This is followed by Latinas at 42.65 percent and white women at 36.4 percent.

We all live in this world together. So why are black people leading the way in unhealthy lifestyles, obesity-related illness, and early death? It's suicide. Our wounds in this area are self-inflicted. We have bought into the lie that tell our black women they are more appealing or curvier when they are heavier. This is a lie, because having curves has nothing to do with being overweight. Our bodies are naturally beautiful if we stay active and feed ourselves for life. The slave food of yesterday has been renamed "soul food" and marketed as a staple of the African American diet. We have bought into this lie by continuing to serve these foods while knowing that a high fat, high red-meat diet leads to diabetes, high blood

pressure, and heart disease, which is the leading cause of death

among African Americans. We have also bought the lie that

African Americans, especially women, should not have to be

active. We have labeled certain sports such as volleyball and

lacrosse as "white sports" and have thus lessened the chances

of having a healthy weight, because we remain inactive.

And what about the children? The matriarchs of the

black family are the ones who are historically cooking and

serving the meals for the family. If they are obese and engage

in unhealthy food choices with no portion control, what are we

teaching our children? Since 1980, childhood obesity rates

nationwide have tripled, and obesity rates for teenagers has

quadrupled. Statistically, four out of five overweight

adolescents will become overweight adults. So once again, the

sins of the father are visited upon the sons. The cycle

perpetuates itself, and we will continue to see a downward

spiral in the health of our race unless we begin to believe that

we are in control of our own futures. Unless we make some

changes to our lifestyle, we are painting a bleak future for our children.

It's not about the white man. Our financial hardships, family breakdowns, homicide crisis, and obesity epidemic have all been created by our own self-destructive behaviors. We are better than this. We are in more control than we think. We can come out of these slave and crab mentalities if we choose to wake up and get to work.

According to Nielsen surveys, African Americans watch more television per week than any other ethnic group. African Americans also spend about fifty-six hours per month using apps and mobile Internet. With all of this access and time, is there any reason why we could not do more with our time?

- Stop saying you don't have enough money to eat healthy. In 2016, black buying power reached 1 trillion dollars. We are the biggest consumers in America. We buy what we want to buy, and we eat what we want to eat. And the last time I checked, a lean meat sandwich and an apple for lunch was a lot less expensive than a McDonald's combo meal.

- Take a free financial course and learn how to manage money. There are many great resources online that can help you get a handle on everything from opening your first checking account to IRAs and investments.

- Find time to go outside and walk every day, or at least dance to a playlist of your favorite music.

- Access a recipe app that can help you find delicious and nutritious ways to feed your family.

- Stop saying you don't have time to cook. Get your crockpot ready at night. Put some meat and vegetables in it and come home to a good-smelling home-cooked meal.

Our bodies have been created the same since God created Adam and Eve. The causes of obesity have not changed. The major contributors to obesity are inactivity, low consumption of fruits and vegetables, and overconsumption of processed food (red meats). We cannot blame the fast food industry or the FDA. While it is true that there is more junk food marketing in black neighborhoods, no one is putting a gun to our heads and making us eat it. During the times of slavery, black families were given the most undesirable and unhealthy cuts of meat to eat, and we turned it into something appetizing and wonderful. But now that we have access to all foods, we have the option to be just as creative in getting our families to eat fruits, vegetables, and lean meats. Believe me—we can turn this around. We have the time, the intelligence, and the resources. All we need is action.

Luke 16:10-11: Whoever can be trusted with very little can also be trusted with much, and whoever is dishonest with very little will also be dishonest with much. So if you have not been trustworthy in handling worldly wealth, who will trust you with true riches?

Chains

A pastor told a story the other Sunday about circus elephants. He said that when the circus elephants are very young, their legs are chained to the ground and they are taught to stand still in their spaces. As the elephants grow and become accustomed to their surroundings, their chains are released. However, the elephant, thinking that their leg is still chained, stays in the spot in the manner in which was trained. Sometimes, our minority communities need to be told that their chains have been released. We must not continue to bleed to death from the wounds we have suffered. Instead, we can apply the pressure of prayer and activism to those areas where we are cut the deepest. We can clean the wound by discussing the issues to help change our minds about how we have defined ourselves. We can bandage the wound by seeking to educate and protect our children and by encouraging them to make positive life decisions. And we can monitor our healing by giving back to those who are trying to get out of poverty, trying to rebuild after incarceration, or trying to hold their families together and need resources and support. Through prayer and activism, we can turn the hurts we have suffered as a people into our areas of greatest strength.

Five Mind-sets That Hold African Americans Back

It has been said that African Americans possess a crab mentality. What it essentially means is that, while some are progressing, others are working to pull that person down into a state where all will eventually perish. But where did this mentality come from, and how can we overcome it?

Perhaps if we are to find the answers, we need to examine our history in America. African Americans are descendants of enslaved Africans. And because of this, we have a mind-set that lines up with the mindset of a slave.

- Slaves see themselves as inferior. From the gladiators of ancient Rome to the lynching of the modern day, enslaved people throughout history have been subjected to violence, humiliation, and buffoonery at the hands of their captors. Today in America, 94 percent of unnatural deaths of African Americans are caused by other African Americans. According to the Bible, "As one thinketh in his heart, so is he." (Proverbs 23:7) Could it be that we have adopted the mindsets imposed upon us long ago? What about the widespread use of the "N" word amongst African Americans? This word, imposed upon us in hatred, has now become a term we treasure and defend in our communities. Someone please tell me why US Koreans make 8 billion dollars a year selling hair weaves to African American women? And why are some of our dress trends so degrading? In our communities, why has it historically been seen as a status symbol for an African American male or female to date or marry someone outside of their race? And what, pray tell, is good hair? We must, somehow, individually throw off these mindsets if we are ever to progress as a people.

- Slaves choose ignorance over knowledge. Frederick Douglas said it best when he stated, "I found that to make a contented slave, it is necessary to make a thoughtless one." A slave, irrespective of race, is defined as "a person conditioned to quietly and without objection accept harmful circumstances for themselves as the natural order of things." African Americans watch two hours more TV per day and play three hours more video games per day than other races. Because of this media exposure, liquor, cigarette, and fast food moguls have increased their marketing to African American youth. Subsequently, African Americans have higher instances of obesity and lifestyle-related deaths than other communities. What about our political ideas? Many of us are still faithful to the welfare systems, and support lawmakers who will uphold them, although this system has demolished our families, punished us for getting an education, and has created an entire culture of unwed mothers and fatherless children. We somehow bought into the same lie that convinced our ancestors not to rebel or escape. We choose our ignorance at the cost of our own souls.

- Slaves are paralyzed by fear. In 2015, black buying power reached 1.1 trillion dollars. African American women are the nation's fasted growing group of entrepreneurs, up 322 percent since 1997. Yet, less than 2 percent of them will become millionaires. Why? I submit that it is fear. Somehow the deep-seated lies of "They will only let you get so far" and "Don't forget where you came from" have creeped from the shadows of slavery into our offices and boardrooms. We also see the effects of this mindset on black business. Many black businesses have been forced to close their doors because they lacked the support of the community they opened to serve. With over a trillion dollars in buying power, blacks still choose to remain the consumers rather than the suppliers.

- Slaves don't free themselves. Martin Luther King Jr. once said, "As long as the mind is enslaved, the body can never be free." We know how to send our children to school, and even to college, but we have failed in teaching our children how to think. The African American community will never thrive if we continue to accept only the history taught in our public schools. We must seek and own our own truth about history, finances, family, and society. We must expose the myths in our thinking and our actions if we ever hope to walk a different road as a people.

Misplaced Priorities

When Johnny Gets in Trouble . . .

We have all heard stories of young men and women who have made poor decisions and ended up in prison. But little is said about the consequences one bad decision will have on the whole family. We know that the loved ones of inmates suffer the separation of their family. They are no longer in the home to raise their children or provide income to support them.

We know that families worry about their loved ones in prison and suffer the grief of regret and broken dreams. But little is said about the back-breaking financial strain families of inmates bear that is both personal and systemic. When Johnny gets in trouble, the whole family gets in trouble with him.

According to the September 2015 edition of *Thinking Progress*, Carlos Gonzalez faced five life sentences for attempting to smuggle five people illegally across the border from Mexico. He was spotted and chased by border patrol, where he crashed his car, killing all of its passengers. His parents were able to refinance the apartment building they owned, while his sisters held fundraisers and asked other family members and loved ones for money. They were able to put together 100,000 dollars to hire the best lawyer possible for his case. Because of this, his sentence of five consecutive life sentences was reduced to thirty years.

Once Gonzalez entered the penal system, he was moved around almost yearly from penitentiary to penitentiary. On average, the facilities were two to four hours away from the family's residence. In order to visit their son on a bimonthly basis, his parents purchased a car that would accommodate the family.

Often times, this meant being ready at 3:00 a.m. in order to be at the facility in time for his visitation hour. During the travel, the family had to purchase food and gas, as well as bring money to eat with while at the facility. The family would bring 125 dollars in singles to the facility so that they could share a meal together. The food was horrible and expensive. A hamburger warmed in the microwave was 6 dollars. But their son was only able to eat the food provided in the vending machines at the prison. So, they all ate there together.

While serving his sentence, Gonzalez's family did everything they could to keep his spirits high and to foster communication. Every three months, they paid the prison 400 dollars for a package of toiletries and clothes. They sometimes paid up to 17 dollars for a fifteen-minute collect call from their son. They paid 32 dollars on occasion to get him small snack items such as Ramen noodles, pop tarts, pickles, and Oreos. For his birthday, they paid 16 dollars to order him a double cheeseburger, fries, and a Coke. At Christmas, they sent care packages that included two packs of Starburst, a six pack of Crush soda, and small packages of peanuts, pretzels, mac and cheese, and potato chips. The family knew that these items their son received would cost one-third to half of this amount in any grocery store, but there were no other options. If they wanted to send email, they could pay 10 dollars for forty letters. If they wanted to send 25 dollars to their son, they were charged additional 6 dollars by the prison system. They paid 20 dollars to purchase him a bag each of Doritos, Cheez-its, and Chex Mix. His parents were unable to retire, his sisters had to readjust their plans for college, and this one poor decision continues to drain the pockets and the heart.

The Ella Baker Center for Human Rights conducted a survey of 368 families of inmates across fourteen states. According to the survey, two-thirds of families said that their financial stability was damaged by the incarceration of their loved one. One-half of these families had also lost one-half or more of their family's income when their loved one went to jail. One-third of families had gone into debt to phone calls and visitation. On average, the court fees each family incurred were 13,607 dollars.

There are two important lessons to be learned from the story of Carlos Gonzalez. First, we must understand that our decisions affect more than just ourselves. When a person goes to jail, their families become wards of the system as well. Secondly, a person whose loved one is facing jail time should spend any money they have up front. If they can raise money, they should raise it to hire the best lawyer possible before the sentence is given. This may make a big difference in the amount of time their loved one will stay behind bars. If they choose to allow a public defender to try the case, the family will almost certainly spend more money over the years that their loved one will spend in prison. So, do yourself and your mother a favor—stay out of this system.

Priorities

My spouse had a very interesting conversation at work the other day. It was back to school season. The children were preparing for a new year, and the parents were preparing for a new schedule.

As the coworkers rolled in, they began to talk about all that they were doing to get their children ready for the upcoming school year. This included hundreds to thousands of dollars in designer clothes, sneakers, and school supplies. Later that day, one of the coworkers began to speak about how her daughter was behind in reading. She asked my spouse about curriculum and about how much it might cost to get her child some extra help. However, upon hearing that tutoring would run her from 100 to 200 dollars a month, her response was, "Wow." Then she changed the subject.

According to a *Business Times* article (August 5, 2017), the average family will spend 501 dollars this year on back to school shopping. About 85 percent of that shopping will be for clothes, shoes, and electronics. The other 15 percent will be for paper, pencils, and supplies and so on. Additionally, parents are expected to spend another 617 dollars over the course of the school year on clothes, especially if their child is involved in sports. These figures are consistent, no matter what income bracket the family falls into, with lower income families actually being on the high end of average spending. However, these expenditures are much different when it comes to how much families spend on tutoring and enrichment educational programs for their children.

Know Better Do Better

According to MIT economics professor Michael Greenstone, "High-income families spend as much as 9,000 dollars annually on private tutoring, SAT prep courses, computers, and other activities, compared with about 1,300 dollars for low-income families."

These are staggering, because according to the *Daily Mail*, "America's poorest families spent over 60 percent of their income on clothing, food, and housing last year." This is a classic case of misplaced priorities. So, let me get this straight. According to the numbers, lower-income families are going into debt, spending money on clothes, shoes, and phones for their children.

They are much less likely, however, to spend the 25 dollars an hour it would take for their children to take weekly tutoring classes to catch up or advance academically.

This is a sad state of affairs. And once again, the children will suffer for the sins of the parents. What kind of message are we sending to our children, when we would rather spend our money trying to make them look like something at school than to help them actually become something at school? Why do so many of our parents cry broke when our children need to purchase an extra book or school supply, yet walk around with 700-dollar iPhones in our pockets? The fact is that we spend money on what we feel is important. No matter how broke we are, we can always find money for the things we prioritize. That being said, we as a people really need to check our priorities. We are so much more than clothes and shoes. We need to teach our kids how important they are to us by providing them with the resources they need to truly succeed, not just in the popularity contest, but in the long run and in the things that really matter. At the end of the day, it will mean nothing that they had expensive shoes and clothes for school if they were unprepared to compete in the game called life.

More Big Problems

Do you not know brothers that you can't kill one another and then march around with a sign and a t-shirt saying, "Black Lives Matter"? I am so tired of turning on the news every day to see that one of our brothers has killed someone or has been killed. Every weekend, there are multiple shootings in black neighborhoods. Our youth are unable to process this kind of grief and heartache and, as a result, have settled into lives of low expectations. They feel that as long as they are living, they are doing alright. We cannot blame "the man" for this one. We cannot blame the police for this one. The fault is our own.

Big problems need big solutions. Let's start with the issue of education. Education should not be left in the hands of the school system. It is ludicrous to think that a child that was left uneducated and undisciplined until the age of five will automatically begin to excel once they enter school. The bad attitude, laziness, and disrespect that they learned in their formative years will begin to play out in their work habits, peer group, and attitude. You have done your child a disservice to let him or her go into school behind the curve. Statistics show that they will remain behind the curve unless someone takes drastic action to catch them up. When the student is young and failing in school, and you do not stop them and you don't want them home because of their disrespect and laziness, where are they to turn? They will then need to know that there are two options. They must return to school and solicit extra help or go to work. If you let them sleep all day and hang out with their friends all night, you have given them a date with disaster. And at the end of the day, when you are visiting them in a jail cell or at the graveyard, and it will be no one's fault but yours.

Another Reason to Vote

Local governments affect more of your life than you may realize. Everything from how your tax dollar is spent to how many police patrol your neighborhoods is affected by local governments. In addition, voter turnout in local elections is often low. Your one vote could literally change the face of your community. And don't forget visibility. Knowing who your local elected officials are gives you a voice when there are issues regarding education, police presence, and even the passing of new laws, and it could be done simply by making a phone call or by having a conversation in the local Walmart.

What you may not know is that the mayor and the board of education are elected positions. However, the school superintendent and the chief of police are appointed positions. The chief of police is appointed by the mayor and city council, and the school superintendent is appointed by the board of education. We cannot complain about the police chief not hiring minorities or limited police presence if we never bothered to vote for the mayor or city council. How can we have a voice in how our teachers are hired or how are schools are performing if we never bother to vote for the school board representatives? In conclusion, educational spending, tax money allocation, public safety issues, roadwork, traffic, and general information about community services are your rights. You should know them, and actively participate to have your voice heard and acknowledged. All you have to do is go out there and vote.

Pull Up Your Pants!

It is said that the origin of wearing saggy pants can be traced to prison life. Inmates are not allowed to have belts in jail owing to the risk of self-hanging or being used as a weapon. This, coupled with the limited availability of sizes, left inmates often wearing ill-fitting pants that sagged at the waistline. However, since the mid-nineties, this fad has become a fashion trend for young men on the outside. Not only is it disrespectful, but it is a form of nudity. No self-respecting man should ever want to show other men their underwear. It is also said that sagging pants are a homosexual signal of availability in the jail. Why would anyone who calls himself a man want any association with something so effeminate? One may see this fad as a simple means of youth expression, yet it is deeper than that. This means of expression is self-degrading at its very core. First of all, it inhibits proper walking and makes you look like a fool in the streets. It signals to others that you are a thug. You couldn't possibly hold a job coming to work with your pants on the ground, so it also is a signal of ignorance. It shows others that you have no respect for them or for yourself, as you would literally show your butt to the world. Come on people! We are better than this!

"Plenty of fashions adopted by young people get under the skin of adults, but the opposition to sagging often has the feel of a moral panic."

—Gene Demby

Unblind Justice

Opinions are opinions, and people will always have them. Some people think Coke is better than Pepsi. Some people prefer mountains to rivers. And some people prefer meat and potatoes to salad and fruit. But once an opinion is formed, it usually stays pretty fluid from person to person. Where I have a problem is when people form and then change their opinions on the basis of the people involved.

Let's take the Bill Cosby and Brett Kavanaugh cases for instance. Hell, let's even throw in Donald Trump for good measure. I am sure we all know that it is wrong to inappropriately or forcibly touch another human being. However, we all must form our own opinions as to whether or not a poor choice made thirty years ago should hinder a person from progressing in their careers or, even worse, send them to jail. Now, once we have formed that opinion, we need to stick with it regardless of who commits the offense.

It seems that Bill Cosby has now been convicted and sent to prison on the basis of accusations from a number of women, one of which admitted that she had been paid to assist in ruining his reputation and legacy. The public outcry has been to lock him up, although he is now eighty-one years old and legally blind. In court, his public label officially changed from "America's dad" to a "violent sexual predator." He now sits in prison, disgraced, confined, ruined.

While all of this is taking place, another series of unfortunate events is taking place. Supreme Court nominee Brett Kavanaugh is accused by several women of sexual assault. The women were interviewed, and statements taken, yet the vote is still set to confirm Mr. Kavanaugh to a lifetime appointment to the highest court in the land. Can we say double standard?

Now, while all of this is taking place, yet another series of events continues to linger on the back pages of newspapers. This is the ongoing accusation of sexual assault committed by President Donald Trump. During Trump's campaign for office, at least twelve women came forward to accuse the then presidential hopeful of sexual assault and illicit affairs. Officers in his own camp have admitted to paying money to women in exchange for their silence concerning their relationships with Trump. Additionally, by Trump's own admission, he was recorded saying that since he was a star, he could "do anything" to women and they would let him. However, somehow and in some way, the voices of the women calling for justice have been silenced, no charges have been filed, and this candidate is now in the White House.

Know Better Do Better

What do we say to these things? Have the eyes of blind justice somehow taken a peek to the color of those to which the laws apply? After all, Cosby, Kavanaugh, and Trump are all wealthy successful men with history and influence in their respective fields. However, it seems to me that the sins of Trump and Kavanaugh are often dismissed by other politicians, the Republican party, and even the public as youthful and foolish, while those of Bill Cosby have been rendered violent and criminal. Trump and Kavanaugh are moving upward in their lives despite the crimes of their past, while Bill Cosby will most likely die in jail.

Can somebody please help me understand? Help me understand why Trayvon Martin rests in heaven while his murderer signs autographs for people on bags of Skittles? Help me understand why so many unarmed black men have lost their lives to police shootings and almost all the shooters have been acquitted. Help me understand why after white racist nationalists stormed Charlottesville, Virginia, the president's response was applauded by the KKK. If Cosby actually did what he was accused of, then justice was served. But justice is supposed to be blind and fair. If Cosby is in a jail cell, then Brett Kavanaugh and Donald Trump should be his cellmates. This is just another instance of the sickening white privilege that makes us take a knee at football games. These kinds of double standards make me sad at what kind of country we are living in and pray for a miracle of a better tomorrow.

The Fleecing of the Poor

When we think of the poor, we think of people who don't have very much money, people who cannot afford the necessities, let alone the luxuries of life. However, here in America, we have a reverse Robin Hood campaign, which robs from the poor and gives to the rich. This campaign is completely legal and going on right under our noses. According to a recent article by Chelsea White, the author of *Five Ways the Poor Pay More Everyday*, the poor pay more in five major ways. First of all, the poor generally pay more for grocery and household items. Many poor families cannot afford to buy necessities such as toilet paper and paper towels in bulk, because although the overall expenditure would be less, the upfront expenditure is more. In a household where money is extremely tight, the upfront cost matters. There is no wiggle room to pay more for toilet paper when there are other needful things to buy, even if it would mean a greater savings in the long run.

The second way that poor families pay more is in transportation. Without reliable transportation, many of our nation's poorest working citizens are forced to pay for public transportation or rely on rides to get to and from work. This often equates to paying a daily rate to bus companies or ride-share services. This is not counting the added cost of buying staple items such as milk and bread at the local convenience stores, which always charge at least a dollar more for these items than at the grocery store.

Another way that the poor are getting robbed in this country is through check cashing, late payments, and fees. While some would say that these are poor choices made by people who should really know better, I would argue that, in many of these cases, there is really no choice at all. Let's take a hypothetical person and name him John. John is a young man who is working a minimum wage and paying half the rent in an apartment. He does not have a car. There is no bank in his neighborhood, but there is a convenience store that offers check cashing for a fee. When John makes his check, he cashes it, pays his half of the rent and bills, buys food for the apartment, and puts some away to pay for the bus the following week. Since he does not have a car, he has paid at least 5 percent just to have his check cashed at the convenience store. He then buys groceries from there, which will cost another 20 percent more than they would have if he could drive to the grocery store. On top of that, he must use a third-party service with fees attached to pay his utility and cell phone bills in cash since he does not have a checking account. Finally, John comes home, with much less of his money to work with than he should have, and another long week ahead. Well, you may be convinced that much of John's problems could be solved by having a car and a checking account. But consider this. A person with a low income and poor credit will almost always pay significantly more for a car than a person with higher income, good credit, and/or cash on hand. So, John would then have an added monthly bill hanging over his head for the next two to five years. And what about the checking account? Most banks have at least a 15-dollar monthly fee attached to the maintenance of a checking account. There are two ways to get around this fee that most people (who are not poor) receive without a second thought. These ways are to maintain a 1500 dollars monthly balance or have direct deposit. Would this be advantageous for John, who would then be faced with getting to and from the bank, paying ATM fees, and keeping a minimum balance? I have known people who went to great lengths to stop a direct deposit because the account had somehow become overdrawn and the direct deposit would end up eaten by bank fees. The 5 dollars that John is paying to cash his check and maintain some control of his hard-earned dollars might now make a little more sense.

Let's talk about time for a moment. Poor people pay more in their time investments than those who make more money. A poor family may have to spend their entire Saturday between the laundromat, the grocery store, and the bus stop. These same errands may take a higher income family only one hour, as they can drive to the grocery store and have their laundry washing at home while they are gone. Lower incomes may often mean that one or both wage earners must either pick up extra hours or work a second job. Finally, the stress of choosing which bills to pay and incurring late payments and credit hits can also increase the time that the poor must spend just trying to make ends meet.

Everyone knows it is cheaper to buy than to rent. So why do so many poor people never get the opportunity to become homeowners? They may have poor credit because of late bill payments. If the housing cost decreased, they would have more money to cover their bills. Right? But sadly, that is not how this country works. Those who already have money, have the greatest opportunity to make more money, and thus have greater opportunities for advancement than poor people. There is even an underhanded strategy called "gapping," which is aimed at using college scholarship money as an incentive for those who can already afford to pay for college, instead of giving it to students who could not attend without the scholarship funds.

Everybody knows that payday loans are a bad idea. In fact, they have been called the "Devil's deals for the dumb and desperate." Yet these establishments are placed disproportionately in poor neighborhoods, luring poor working-class citizens with false promises. Eviction, sickness, or even the shutting off of utilities can create feelings of discouragement and desperation for the working poor. Sometimes, situations can get so desperate that even short-term relief, with strings attached, can look like an oasis.

So, it seems that everywhere we look, we see instances where the working poor in this country are robbed of their time, money, and stability thanks to these legal tactics that allow the privileged to get over and make money off the backs of our most vulnerable citizens. Welcome to the American dream.

Why Are Black Youth Leaving the Church?

There is so much going on in the world today, and people are looking for answers. All people, especially young people, are looking to make sense of the issues that are on the forefront of our newspapers, hearts, and minds. But it seems that fewer people are looking to the church as a source of the answers they so desperately need. In this chapter, we will explore some of the reasons why the church is losing ground and discuss solutions to return our youth to the true source of strength and encouragement.

According to a September 8, 2013, article in the Voice Magazine, African American youths have become disengaged by the "Euro-centric" framework of the Christian church. The world, in reality, is plagued by racial turmoil. More often than not, the African American is placed at the bottom of the totem pole in opportunities that lead to achievement and economic success. The Bible states truly that we are all from "one blood," yet this truth is rarely lived out in the world, even in Christian circles. Some have said that Sunday morning is still the most segregated day of the week, and by and large, it is. White Christians and black Christians attend their various services each week, yet no desperately needed change takes place in the fibers of our culture. Many of our youths are asking why. African American youth are looking for a place to affirm their identity and their ethnicity as important and relevant. They are also looking for a real-time explanation for the racism and hatred that so heavily permeates the American society. Where is God in all of this chaos, and how can a Christian understand and combat these evils while still staying true to what they believe? Christianity is also losing ground to the nation of Islam in our prison system. Due to such issues as low morale, protection, and rejection of the "system," many African American men who enter the prison system convert to Islam on the inside. Why is this a common occurrence, and what can be done to win the lost and hurting to the one true God?

While some blame the negative issues of modern life for our youth's lack of belief, other sources paint a very different picture. According to the January 1, 2014, issue of the *Atlanta Black Star*, the economic and social benefits now enjoyed by many African American youths have made the need for faith less prevalent. Though there are many problems in the world, millennials are enjoying a wealth of information and opportunity through the Internet and social media that their parents never imagined. There are forums and chat rooms and opinions on so much that many young people do not feel the need to connect with a local church as a source for answers. They feel they can find it themselves. This also leads to the argument of intellect versus faith. In today's world, youth are ready to have real conversations that ask tough questions. Where do they go when they are wrestling with doubt concerning their lives, identity, and future? And if they do come to us, is the church ready to answer these questions with love, encouragement, and acceptance?

In 2007, 83 percent of all African Americans referred to themselves as Christians. Now in 2017, only ten years later, those numbers have dropped significantly. According to Gallop polls, the number of African Americans as a whole who refer to themselves as Christians is now only 78 percent, with the numbers dropping to only 62 percent for Africans Americans aged eighteen to twenty-nine. The last two documented reasons for the decline in Christian belief are those that run deep in our culture and have been swept under the rug for way too long. How do African Americans make peace with the religion that was used as a source of control and slavery for over four hundred years? How do we reason with the fact that we were told for centuries that black people were meant to be slaves and servants, and that the Bible backed that up? How do we move forward in Christ and still fight for our social justice and change? The last major issue that must be confronted by the church is that of authenticity. Gallop polls have shown that although the Bible teaches against sex outside of marriage, Christian singles are just as sexually active as their non-Christian counterparts. Christian youths struggle with sexuality, peer pressure, drug abuse, pornography, and bullying just like everyone else. However, for many Christians, their struggles also come with fear, shame, hiding, and judgment. Many youths raised in Christian homes and churches struggle with the mediocre or hidden lives lived by their parents or those in Christian leadership. They feel that not only is there a lack of answers to some of life's toughest questions, but that there is also a lack of acknowledgement that these issues exist in Christian arenas. Because of this facade, the help for these needs goes unmet.

We, as the church, must first be a place of love. Without love, those who need God will not seek Him. No one wins when shame is present. And the Jesus I know does not condemn those who are willing to come and be healed. Secondly, the church must acknowledge that the struggles we all face are real. Racism, sexism, and social, familial, economic, and internal struggles come knocking at all of our doors, and neither the saint nor the sinner is exempt. This thing called life, instead of being a divider, could instead be the thing that helps us to unite and grow together. Lastly, we as the church need to lose religion and focus on relationship in real time. What is our purpose for being born on this earth? What does it really mean to be saved? And how is my life different because of a relationship with God? I think he Voice Magazine puts it best when it says, "If the church wants to reach disillusioned and disenfranchised youth, one of the things it should do is equip young believers to tackle problems. It needs to speak their language, understand their struggles and help them overcome them. Secondly, the church needs to be heard speaking about the issues that concern young men like racism, poverty, inequality, and unemployment. Thirdly, it has to share the gospel in a way that reflects their reality, offers the God as the remedy, and follows through with love."

Twenty-Four Reasons Why It Is Hard for Us to Get Ahead

1. The grand idea of capitalism is that if those with capital will apply it to create more wealth, that will lead to more jobs and income for everyone. Not only will the wealth benefit them, but their wealth will trickle down to the common man. This is good in theory but in recent times, wealth is more likely to trickle up. The wealthy have become better off, and the gap is growing between the rich and the poor people in this country. And the future looks grim, as the rich continue to use their wealth to lobby Congress to write more laws that benefit the rich, in exchange for a large campaign donation.

2. What we want is hope and opportunity in this thing we call the "American Dream." But what we mostly get is capitalist greed.

3. We have the time and the resources. What we need are commitment and hard work.

4. Most of the time, common sense brings common solutions.

5. The pen is mightier than the sword, and the one with the gold makes the rules.

6. This is a rough world, just waiting for you to come unprepared, so it can chew you up and spit you out.

7. Poor people don't have tax loopholes. Most tax breaks present a clear advantage for the rich. With those tax loopholes, the rich get richer. Those tax breaks equate to over a trillion dollars in losses for the government. Politics aligns with big business, and the wealth stays at the top.

8. Warren Buffett says that rich people should leave their children and grandchildren enough money to do something, but not enough to do nothing.

9. There is a big difference between what we are doing and what we should be doing. Pointing fingers is hopeless. Real change takes effort.

10. Big business has taken the attitude that any and everything is acceptable in the pursuit of profit. They will lay off thousands of American workers and outsource the jobs to other countries. They cut our

heads off and hand it to us, and then say, "It's just business."

11. People will say that you can't beat the system. Many believe that if you were born poor, you will always be poor, and that's the way it is. Well, I was born and raised in poverty, and I don't believe that. Neither did Dr. King when he said, "If you are behind in a race, that just means you have to run that much faster." According to the US Census Bureau, more than 43.6 million Americans live in poverty.

12. Tavis Smiley and Cornell West have taken this a step further in their claims that one in every two Americans lives in poverty. By this, they include both those who earn low incomes and those who live paycheck to paycheck.

13. A family of four is considered poor if the family income is less than 23,850 dollars per year. About one-third of Americans experience occasional poverty, and almost 20 percent of Americans live in poverty all the time.

14. The living conditions of the US poor are propped up by food stamps, housing vouchers, welfare payments, social security, and other help.

In my opinion, the US minimum wage is a disgrace. Those opposed to raising the wage cite two possible, undesirable consequences. First, some small businesses may have to close if they cannot afford to pay the higher wage. Secondly, employers will search for other ways to replace their labor force. Both of these consequences happen every day in this country with the wage being as it has been for all these years. There are no guarantees in life or business. However, we should be making the effort to pay our labor force enough money to pay for rent, gas, and food in today's economy.

15. Three major problems facing our country today are middle class, stagnation, the growing gap between in incomes between the rich and the poor, and poverty.

16. One of the best ways to solve our poverty problem is to help ourselves and our families move away from a poor mindset.

The growing income disparity is not only a disaster for the rich but is also a threat to the poor. Poverty breeds broke families, low test scores, crime and criminal organization, prostitution, drug dealing, and other acts of desperation. No one is immune to the effects of poverty.

17. Do you know how long the minimum wage has been 7.25 dollars in this country? My question is, why didn't you know that? Are you that far removed from the problem, or do you feel that you have your wealth and others have theirs to get?

18. We have to look further ahead than where we are today. The future is imminent, and we must learn to manage it. At some point, many realize that they are in a rat race for higher income. They are not only keeping up with the Joneses, but now they want to do better than them as material possessions go. We have become the Joneses in wealth, but not in net worth. There is a difference.

In 2010, the Republican House, under the influence of

the tea party, cut the US Internal Revenue Service (IRS) budget by 14 percent, resulting in a sharply reduced staff, less tax enforcement, and weaker taxpayer services. In 2010, the IRS was able to audit 30 percent of taxpayers. Yet in 2013, it could only audit 24 percent of taxpayers. This means that the government collected less revenue for roads, clean air, water, healthcare, and other vital tasks. The Republicans also push constantly for lower taxes for the rich on the premise that people need a strong incentive to work hard. This is just another way for the rich to make all the money they can. It is all about the money.

19. Most of the money politicians receive comes from those who are wealthy rather than those who are middle class. Politicians often have little choice but to carry out the requests of the rich and vote for what the wealthy want.

20. I don't know why the rich are complaining about high taxes. They have lawyers that find so many loopholes and deductions that they get out of paying many of the taxes that the middle class and working poor must pay.

21. High incomes can come from having the right parents. If you are born into a wealthy family, you have an advantage. You have the opportunity to go to the right colleges, hire tutors, and spend your time in the library instead of at a part-time job. You may even land that great job thanks to family connections. It happens every day.

22. There will always be an extreme difference in income. This is called survival of the fittest, and it manifests in different ways.

23. The rich have raced far ahead of the middle class and the poor and are steadily rising. In 2012, the income of the top 1 percent of wage earners in the country rose nearly 20 percent, compared to a 1 percent increase in income for the remaining 99 percent.

24. There is a growing concern about income inequality. The high level of youth unemployment has triggered social protests, but no real change.

There are those who try to justify income inequality by saying, "The rising tide lifts all the boats." Well, it seems that only the boats of the rich are being lifted by the rich, and the rest of us are sinking.

Income and Education

One of the most significant factors influencing high school dropout rates is family income. According to the US Department of Education, students from low-income families are six times more likely to drop out of high school than students from high-income families. What is the state's role? Many of the most significant factors affecting dropout rates, like family income, are beyond the reach of the school system. There are programs such as Project Graduation and Race to GED to support or aid students who are considering dropping out or who may have dropped out already.

So, is a student at risk for dropping out of school just because they come from a poor family? Does family income have anything to do with a person's intelligence? Does family income affect a person's ability to listen and retain information, solve an equation, or write a paper? Absolutely not! The answer most likely lies in failing schools, limited resources, and lack of advocacy.

In Virginia, there are nine high schools where the dropout and late graduation rates are 33 percent or higher. These schools follow a trend of poverty and dense minority populations. Where are the parents, teachers, principals, and school board members who will advocate for these and other schools across the nation? We need meaningful resources to help these schools reach standards. Loss of accreditation cannot be the only answer, because when these schools lose their accreditation, the students who lack the funds and resources to go to a "successful" school are left sitting on a sinking ship. In these cases, parents, especially minority parents, need to attend school board and PTA meetings. Above all, they need to be visible, letting our students know that their future is important, and they have the support of friends and family members. If there are academic problems, families should seek the assistance of tutors. This is a country bursting with opportunity. We cannot continue to tell our children to play the hand they are dealt. The cards are unfairly distributed, and minorities need to advocate for a reshuffle.

Why Smart People Do Dumb Things (With Their Money)

A person goes to the grocery store to buy a few items. They intend to buy milk, eggs, frozen waffles, and bacon. They purchase the milk, eggs, and bacon at the store. Then they remember that another store has frozen waffles on sale for a slightly better price, so they buy their items, get back in the car, and drive five or ten minutes to the next store for a slightly better price. Now they do find the frozen waffles on sale for a slightly better price, but they also notice a sale on orange juice and ground beef. At the end of the day, this person has spent twice as much time and money running to the second store as they would have if they had simply bought what they needed from the first one. And they did it all in the name of saving 35 cents.

Another person needs to fill up his or her car at the gas station. There is a station nearby selling gas for an average amount. Yet, the person drives around for fifteen minutes trying to compare prices at various stations throughout the city. At the end of the trip, their gas tank is running on fumes and they have wasted ten minutes waiting in a line to get gas at the cheap station. But hey, at least they saved 6 cents per gallon, which equals about 48 cents per fill-up.

What about the people who make an average salary and place it in the bank? Over time, their savings grow, yet they keep their money in the same bank account, at the same bank year after year. Why not stop in and talk to the bank about the programs where that same money could earn interest at a much higher rate than a traditional savings or checking account? Did you forget that the banks should work for you and not the other way around?

Finally, don't buy another timeshare. It's just like the one you already have. You don't get that much time off and you're not using it anyway.

So, You Want to Be a Millionaire!

There are thousands of books out there that say they can tell you how to be a millionaire. Some say you can get there by selling real estate. Some say you can get there by using your 401k and 403B. Some say you can get there by way of the stock market. Others say you can use mutual funds and other get-rich-quick programs. While there are some good books out there, frankly, most are not worth the paper they are written on. That is why this book is not about any of those things. This book is different. It's about moving forward to take that next step. It's about being better than you are right now. It's about taking one step at a time to move one step ahead. This book is about looking out for yourself and your family. It's about forward mobility. This book is about giving you a hand up and not a handout. It is about teaching you how to fish. It's about making your dreams come true. This book is about more than money. It is about your kids getting great education, going to better schools, living in better neighborhoods, and having better opportunities. This book is about living the life you should live.

The first thing we need to do is spend less than we make. If that is not possible right now, we then look for ways to increase what we make. We can do that by working overtime, working on our days off, asking for hours from our coworkers, or getting a part time job. Then we need to devise a plan for the extra money we make. That extra money does not mean new cars, clothing, or household items. But how do you save? Well, you have to have a goal in mind. Make a plan, set some goals, and execute. Imagine yourself moving forward and work hard for yourself.

Stop Procrastinating!

One thing is for sure—time waits for no man. No one can be sure just how much time they have to accomplish the things on their to-do list before life happens, or worse, death happens, and those dreams fly away forever. It never ceases to amaze me that everyone thinks they have more time than they actually have. Although we are all aware that that life can come to an end without warning, we never think that *it* will happen to us. And because we never think anything will happen to derail our plans, we procrastinate. Well, I'll let you in on a secret. Life will pass you by. You may think that you have all the time in the world to start that business, write that book, or get that education, but in actuality, you don't. God gives each man a finite number of days and often an even smaller window of opportunity to accomplish his goals before age, illness, or other life circumstances rearrange our priorities. The best thing I can tell you is to stop waiting and take steps now to accomplish the dreams in your heart.

Some of us are looking to build wealth and save money for our children's education. We rationalize when they are young that college is so far away, and besides, we don't have the money to invest because our money is being spent on diapers and daycare. But if we are not careful, college time will creep up on us, and if we have not invested, we could be forced to assume more debt, or worse, place the financial burden of college squarely on our children's backs. It's not what we would have wanted, but often, that is the way things turn out when we assume that time is on our side.

Others of us have a book or other business idea that we are trying to get off the ground. We think we could be successful, but we rationalize that we will do it when the time is right. Meanwhile, we see other people's dreams coming to fruition, and we start to wonder whether we are—I mean, our idea is—good enough. We begin to question and second-guess ourselves about whether the timing is right, whether anyone will want what we have to offer, or whether someone else can do what we do better than we can.

Some of us are simply afraid to invest in ourselves. We are afraid of starting something we can't finish. We are afraid of how people will accept or reject our ideas. And most importantly, we are afraid of the unknown. We are branching out into unfamiliar waters, and we are not sure if we really trust ourselves to see this idea through to the end. I have to be frank. It would be great if a millionaire saw our talent at the ground level and was willing to invest his money into our idea to get it off the ground. However, for most of us, that will never happen.

We will need to invest in ourselves way before anyone will invest in us. We will need to shoulder the financial burden, and we will need to invest the sweat equity before anyone else will offer to help us. Most investors are looking for products and services that are already making money. Even on popular shows such as *Shark Tank*, the investors want to know how much profit the business is already making before they will invest to take the business to the next level. Investing in yourself will be the only way to get things done and get them done right.

I'm here to tell you that there will always be obstacles in your way that try to steal your confidence and shake your resolve. However, if there truly is a calling in your heart, it will continue to nag you even after you have weighed the pros and cons. It will continue to nag you even after you have seen people try and fail. It will continue to call your name, because that is what it is—a calling. Callings are from God and cannot be denied. It does not matter how many books have been written on your topic of choice, your book still needs to be written. No matter how many businesses have been created, crashed, and burned before your very eyes, your business still needs to be born. There are over seven billion people on this earth. You must believe that there is something about how you deliver your service, product, or message that is needed to meet the needs of someone out there. You've got to believe in yourself and in the power of what you have to offer. If not, your dream will follow you to the grave, and the people who need what you have will be underserved. What a waste of a good idea. Stop procrastinating and get to work. You will learn as you go. Start your business now. Start saving for college now. Begin that book now. Now is your moment. Don't waste it.

Chapter Three

Kill the Noise (And Silence the Haters)

Samuel 9:2: Love your brother, your neighbor and your potential enemy... There's an old saying keep your friends close and your enemies closer.

We all have friends that we call strange people. We talk with them, we go out with them, and our kids may even hang out together. We know a little about their house, their car, even their income. What we often do not know is where they work. When asked, they may be vague, change the subject, and indicate that they work with computers and numbers. When you continue to ask, he continuously avoids the subject. These secret friends also have a child in an Ivy League College where the tuition is 40,000 to 50,000 dollars a year where they also want their other child to attend. My point is that you have these friends that seem to know how to make enough money to get the house, the car, the vacations, all while sending their kids to expensive schools. Maybe they know about good investments that have been paying them back for years, or they are building houses or have rental property on the side. My point is that they are your friends and you feel like they should let you in on what they are doing.

Real friends will let you know what they are doing that is successful so that you can grow together. They will want you to join them in their investments and partner with them in their businesses. On the other hand, these secretive associates are not really friends. They don't want to share the secrets to their success, and if you continue to press them for this information, you will soon discover that even the relationship you once had ends and they no longer want to associate with you.

People will try to muddy your water simply because you are trying to work hard to get ahead. While you may see your work as a "need," they look at you and say you are just being greedy. However, there are two things wrong with that statement. The first is that it is your work and your business. The second is that people will always put other people's efforts down in hopes of making themselves feel better about where they are in life. Some people don't want you to work harder than them because it makes them feel bad. However, instead of working harder, they sit back and call you greedy. I say kill the noise.

Stop listening to the haters and do what you need to do to get where you want to be. Life is hard enough in this country without people trying to put stumbling blocks in your way. Can you believe that in 2019 we still have black people with the crab mentality? Well, believe it. People ask me all the time, "Why are you writing a book when you have never written anything in your life?" I have a very simple answer for them. I never saw a need to write something until now. Now that the need is here, it is time for me to pick up the pen. They ask peculiar questions such as, "Do you have time to write a book?" The answer is no. I do not. I have a real estate business that I am trying to run and that keeps me as busy as I want to be.

But I have something to say to my friends and family and those who will come after me. There is nothing wrong with trying to make some extra money and trying to live a better life. My haters can sit there and continue to say that life is great, but in actuality, life seems to be getting harder. I just read that rent prices, owing to the demand in this area, have gone up 18 percent in the last five years. We live in the richest country on earth, but the gap between rich and poor continues to widen with no solutions in sight. The playing field has never been level, but that knowledge cannot be an excuse for us not achieving what others in this country have achieved. As for myself, I am going after my piece of the pie. No one can stop me. My mind is made up. I am going after my dirt and my mortar, and I am not going let some third-party moron talk me out of building up my house. I have said what I mean, and I mean what I have said. The way you get your piece of the pie is just like eating an elephant. It happens one bite at a time. I have to keep in mind that if I don't do it, who will? 1 take full responsibility for where I am and where I am going. I just feel like we need to push ourselves just a little bit harder. We can silence the noise of the haters and continue to reach for the stars.

Throwing in the Towel

"Throwing in the towel" is the phrase we use to describe quitting and refusing to fight anymore. We see it in boxing when one fighter is getting beaten so badly that the representatives from his corner will throw a white towel into the ring to signify that the fighter has had enough and is quitting the match. We also see it in other sports such as baseball and basketball. One team can be winning, but when the points begin to widen to where there is no chance of the other team catching up, the referee can call the game and declare the winner without further upset to the losing team. But life is not like that. You, as the head of your household, cannot throw in the towel. You can't quit just because things are not going well for you. Maybe you can't find a job right now, or maybe you did not get that promotion. Perhaps the banks are still saying no to your business loan, and the plans are going downhill. Understand this. There are a lot of people depending on you. They understand how you get beat up on that so-called "job." They all know that you have been knocked down. But that is not what matters. Your children and family are waiting to see if you are going to get back up. Throwing in the towel is not an option for you. You may feel that you are on a very small island by yourself. This is not true, and even if it were, you have to make your move, because at the end of the day, it is all on you. Ecclesiastes 3:1 states,

"To everything there is a season, and a time to every purpose under the heaven."

If there is one thing I know for sure about life, it is that seasons come and go. Your breakthrough will come through if you do not give up. You will begin to see the light at the end of the tunnel if you keep digging. Keep knocking on doors, and one will eventually open for you.

Be an example to your children, that you stayed in the race and refused to give up. Even if your back hurts when you come home from work, let them see that you go every day to make a better life for them. Do all that you can. Do what you have to do. But, don't do yourself and your family in by giving up.

We all need to have goals. Short- and long-term goals are necessary for every individual. Where will you be next year this time? What about five years from now, or after retirement? Have you calculated the years you have until your child goes to college? Do you know how much that will cost? Are you prepared or preparing for that? Where will the money come from to send your child to become a doctor, lawyer, or an engineer? If you have a goal, you will realize that, in order to accomplish them, you will have to make some sacrifices along the way. You may not be able to afford that new car. Or maybe it is time for you to cut back on some of those items you buy in the store simply because it says "Sale." Most people say they are sacrificing, but in reality, they never reach their long-term goals because they think they can have everything. We have accomplished very little as a people with this self-satisfaction attitude. Now it is time to regroup.

Let me tell you something about money. You have to do more than make money to become wealthy. There are a lot of people out here that look like millionaires. They have great incomes. They have big houses. They have the clothes, the jewelry, the cars, the pool, and the boat. They may have assets that total well over a million dollars. But they are not wealthy. The reason they look like they have a million dollars is because their spending is off the chain. These people have high incomes, but low net worth. This is why as black incomes are rising, our net worth as a people has not. We are not saving any money to invest in the bright futures of our children.

Let me fill you in on a little secret. The money you make may not be your biggest problem. What you do with your money may be the game changer that you need. The best way to make money is to let your money work for you. Instead of investing in cars that quickly depreciate, invest your money in something that will pay you, such as real estate, stocks and bonds, or mutual funds. Don't work harder; work smarter.

Here is another little secret. Just because you are doing alright does not mean you should not try to do better. There is always room for improvement, and as you rise, so will your family's opportunities. In order to save money, we should have a low-consumption lifestyle. Low consumption lifestyles are those where there is money to save after the bills are paid. Also, your net worth has a lot to do with your age. If you are twenty-six years old and you have a net worth of 5000 dollars, that may be good for you. You have 5000 dollars that is not owed to anyone. But if you are fifty-six years old and you have a net worth of 5000 dollars, that is not good. That twenty-six-year-old could invest in riskier and higher yielding opportunities than the fifty-six-year-old and still have plenty of time to make it up if it did not work out. However, the fifty-six-year-old cannot afford to do this because he is too close to retirement.

Saving is not just for those wanting to get rich. Saving is also for poor people who desire to move up into the middle class. Just by virtue of accomplishing that goal to become middle class, you will have a very different voice in America's economy. Politicians sit on platforms all day long and discuss the future of the rich and middle class in our country, yet they seldom ever mention legislation to help the poor. It is as if poor people don't count or don't exist. So, you have two choices. The politicians will not help you. You can vote them out and find a way to help yourself. Most people have money at the end of their bills that they spend on something. All I am asking is for you to believe that financial independence is more important than displaying high social status.

Some food for thought:

Teach your children how to fish. This means that instead of just feeding them, you also teach them how to feed themselves. Teach them the importance of a good education, smart money practices, and economic stability. American millionaires are more than five times more likely than the average household to have a child that will graduate from medical school. They are more than four times more likely to have a child graduate from law school. In this way, future generations are taught how to fish, so that they do not look at their parents as a fish dispensing machine.

Your child does not have to go to an Ivy League college to get a good education. But they should get some type of education or training after high school.

Most successful business owners put much of their own resources behind their ventures. Saving money will open doors for your future.

It's amazing what you can do when you set your mind to it. It's a matter of planning your work, and then working your plan. Be price sensitive when making purchase decisions. Take a positive attitude about yourself. Don't let the naysayers tell you what you can't do. Lastly, saving money will require you to be resourceful and not afraid of hard work. Saving your money to build a better future may require you to live a plain, more simple life. But if you do, there is a great chance that your children will not have to work as hard as you do. They will be well educated and will be able to become what they dream. At the end of the day, your saving and sacrifice will have made it all possible. So, don't give up.

The Cure for Discouragement

Surround yourself with people who are going the way you are going. People who are going someplace. People who want to be somebody. People who want to have something in life. Don't associate with people who don't want anything, because while you are on your way to school or work, they will be a discouragement rather than an encouragement for you. While you are trying to find a way to get promoted on your job, they will tell you how good it is to have no real job responsibilities. There will always be gloom-and-doom people who tell you that the bank will not lend you any money to fund your business, how black people will not support your business, and how you may lose your money. But let me tell you this. Sometimes you will have to motivate yourself. Now I know that I have said this before, but I want to put weight and emphasis on this: Do not get discouraged if your family and friends don't see or understand what you are doing. Don't get discouraged if even the people you are seeking to help do not understand your goals.

You may have to take some people to school. Tell them that they can do better than just doing alright. Let them know that money in the bank is better than new clothes and a new car. Let them know that the storms of life will come, and they need to be prepared or it will rain all over their parade.

No matter how much your critical so-called friends, your naysayers, and haters say you can't do it, you will still have to put one foot in front of the other and keep moving. Nobody said it would be easy. But success will not come to you. You will have to go get it.

To Store or Not to Store

Ecclesiastes 5:13: *There is a grievous evil, which I have seen under the sun: riches being hoarded by their owner to his hurt.*

It is important to be a good servant of our finances. Accumulating excess stuff that you do not use and do not have space for runs counter to saving and managing your resources.

One way that people often waste money because they have collected more "stuff" than they have room to store is the use of long-term storage facilities. You cannot travel more than ten miles without spotting them. There are close to sixty thousand self-storage facilities worldwide, and over 10 percent of all households in the United States maintain one. Storage facilities are everywhere and they have certainly increased in popularity over the past five years.

Although there are an overwhelming number of cons to maintaining a long-term storage unit, there are some cases where a person may need to have one. Often times, you may not have a garage or your garage is damp and prone to mold and mildew. In this case, you may opt to store materials in a climate-regulated storage as opposed to storing them in a garage; however, before taking this option, you should consider how important these items are and how often you need them. Holiday and other seasonal materials can easily be stored in a home closet. Furniture that is not used should definitely be sold. Donate furniture that has not been used in over a year. You can also donate to charity with an added bonus of receiving a tax credit at the end of the year.

Some storage facilities advertise that they are the positive solution to the hoarder or the person who constantly obtains more objects than he does or she can keep in their home. Paying a monthly bill to store materials that do not fit in your house is extremely wasteful. Why not purge materials and keep only those things that you either love or use frequently? Good advice is not even to purchase things you do not absolutely love or that you definitely won't frequently use. I recall Oprah saying how she gives clothes away every time she buys new clothes. This is excellent advice. Why make a monthly payment for something you do not need? These storage fees can be financially draining.

Another good reason not to rent long-term storage is that having the extra space gives you the feeling that you can and should get more stuff to fill them up. Imagine the extra square feet of house you could get with the extra 100 dollars a month you are spending on storage space. Imagine the debt you could pay down with that money and imagine the savings account you could build. Worst-case scenario imagines if for some reason you are unable to make your monthly payment. Your storage unit could become repossessed and you will lose your possessions as well as all the money you have invested in the monthly storage payments.

There are unique situations for which a storage unit may be necessary, for example, you are about to move, or you are renting and purchasing items for a house you are buying in the future, or you move frequently. But each of these instances call for short-term versus long-term storage solutions.

So, if you are hoarding, please stop. You are only hurting yourself.

The Bigotry of Low Expectations

There is a quote I once heard made by George W. Bush, and while I do not know the actual origin of the quote, it has stayed with me throughout the years: "There is a subtle bigotry of low expectations." I am inclined to agree.

Today our youth are faced with not only the need to challenge or defend what they can or cannot do, they must also challenge what people believe they can or cannot do. Unfortunately, for the African American youth, this expectation is usually low, reflecting a subtle and, sadly, often not-so-subtle bigotry. It is amazing that, in this day in time, many African American students still report that their teachers treat them differently, they notice being watched and sometimes even followed in stores, and they feel the humiliation of people clutching their bags and locking doors when they pass. For these youth, low expectations and the accompanying bigotry follow them every day of their lives. Knowing that this problem exists means nothing in the absence of the solution. How do our youth show that they can exceed the expectations that continue to plague them? The answers simplistically begin at home, and the responsibility belongs with parents and guardians. We are fighting an uphill battle, but we must continue to fight.

If the world believes that you are inherently dishonest, prove them wrong by going beyond expectations in the field of trustworthiness and integrity.

Pay Your Bills

African Americans are often negatively stereotyped as horrible financial trustees and are often thought to frivolously spend while avoiding paying bills. Never mind the fact that we just elected a president who has filed bankruptcy over five times, African Americans need to work harder and do better, because fair or not, they will never receive the same forgiveness or passes. We all have the ability to fall on hard times, but we should do everything in our power to change our situation even if it includes multiple jobs and fewer opportunities for fun and entertainment. Don't sit around idly waiting for the government to take away benefits; make a plan toward self-sufficiency.

Hold Children Accountable for Their Actions

The saddest line I read in the paper or hear on the news after the death of a young black person is, "He/she was just getting her life together." We all know that this statement is the code for "My child has made so many mistakes in his life and he may have changed if he had lived longer." While this change was definitely possible, we all know that it was probably not likely. Repeated rule and law violations are not mistakes; they are purposeful attempts to get away with something they didn't earn. As parents, we have to call our children at this point. Yes, we want to help them get through these mistakes, but we also have to make it clear that your expectation is that they don't continue to make them. Our children don't have to work while in high school or college, but the expectation should be that they at least have chores in the house or that they make the highest grades they can. Clothes and things are nice, but it is hard work that makes successful and responsible adults.

Make Education a Priority

By education, I don't just mean high school or college, I also mean worthwhile skills. W. E. B. Du Bois and Booker T. Washington made these arguments close to a hundred years ago, and they still ring true today. Washington argued that students need an industrial education that could lead to economic independence, while Du Bois argued for the importance of college degrees and intellectual experiences. Today, both options can lead to financial growth and independence. With the great demand for skilled workers, a plumber or an engineer can create a lifestyle that rivals or surpasses that of a doctor, lawyer, or PhD candidate. Whether a skill or an education, the only mistake is not pushing our children to acquire one or the other.

Only by ensuring that our children and family members are honest, hardworking, and educated individuals can we combat the bigotry of low expectations.

The Pros and Cons of Public Housing

I am a product of the welfare system. My father, our family's bread winner, passed away when I was a young boy. Shortly after, my mother fell ill. Life was hard and the money she made was often insufficient to meet the needs of seven children. Moving into public housing was truly a step-up for us. It allowed my siblings and myself to focus on school and work, rather than worrying whether we would have a roof over our heads. However, there were also negative aspects of the welfare program that, even today, continue to mar the effectiveness of the program as well as the communities they were developed to serve. This is a conversation that needs to be discussed honestly and objectively in our community.

Public housing initiatives were created after the Great Depression to give senior citizens, the disabled, and fledgling Americans an opportunity to escape homelessness. According to www.thebalance.com, there are six major US welfare programs: Temporary Assistance for Needy Families,

Medicaid, Food Stamps, Supplemental Security Income,

Earned Income Tax Credit, and Housing Assistance. Here, we

will address public housing.

The pros to welfare are pretty self-explanatory. Those

who may otherwise be homeless or starving are given a roof

over their heads. They have the opportunity to feed their

children and be safe indoors, while they work to build their

lives. Seniors citizens and the disabled of our communities are

able to receive a place to live and food to eat. Anyone who has

suffered a job loss, has become disabled, or is on a fixed

income can be eligible for welfare, and each taxpayer pays a

little out of their paycheck to help make this happen. It

absolutely sounds like the right thing for a nation to do.

Yet, the welfare system has a dark side. Over the years,

there has been an increasing number of non-disabled, non-

senior citizen families who have stayed on the welfare system

for years and even generations, with no drive to overcome it. In

2018, the federal poverty level was 25,100 dollars annually for

a family of four. In certain ways, the welfare system has

encouraged women to become single mothers and avoid

marriage in order to stay below the income level, which entitles them to free housing, food, health care, and day care for their children. Quite honestly, there is little incentive to earn an honest living, as even the slightest raise in pay could disqualify a person from thousands of dollars in monthly benefits. Two-income households are virtually non-existent on the program with the income requirements being so low. In response, many fathers are "live-in visitors" rather than productive members of the family. Children in this system are often raised without a clear depiction of the value of work. As a result, many have resorted to other "easy" ways to get money, such as theft and drug dealing. A "get over" spirit emerges as the younger generations learn the system and begin to take advantage of it for themselves.

Is there a middle ground? Could the welfare system be a hand up to some without becoming a handout to others? Are Section 8 vouchers, work requirements, and mixed income housing the answer to concentrated poverty and the problems that often result? Or should the system be done away with altogether and rebuilt from the ground up? Many people have various ideas and perspectives, but I will end this discussion by saying that the welfare system helped my family get on its feet.

Public housing gave us a stable community to grow up in. Yes,

it had its problems, but every one of my brothers and sisters

has gone on to contribute in positive ways to our community as

well as to our nation. You be the judge.

Skills or Education: Choose One Or the Other, but Choose

Booker T. Washington developed programs for job

training and vocational skills at Tuskegee Institute. He stressed

on jobs and training, and he felt that if youth had skills, they

would be able to get jobs from anyone. He believed that black

people should prioritize economic security before obtaining

equality and that equality would come once African Americans

were able to take care of themselves.

W. E. B. Du Bois wanted immediate equality and believed

that the only way to gain this equality was through classical

education acquired through a high school and a college degree.

Currently, the unemployment rate for African

Americans is 8.8 percent, more than double the rate for Whites

at 4.3 percent. Additionally, African Americans are the only

race where the women have a higher employment rate than the

men. Choosing either a vocation or an education can combat this unemployment epidemic.

If you choose a college degree, choose wisely. Although more African Americans are going to college than ever before, the Center on Education and the Workforce at Georgetown University found that the majors students are selecting often lead to low-paying jobs. The best majors are found in STEM and business. Additionally, the study found that even when African Americans major in higher earning degrees, they choose the lowest paying major. Becoming an engineer is a wonderful choice, but many African Americans choose to major in civil engineering, which pays the lowest of all engineering professions. Additionally, African Americans often major in sociology majors that usually pay lower wages and often require an additional graduate degree. According to the US Census, majors in architecture, engineering, computers, math, and statistics begin with earnings above 60,000 dollars. On the other hand, majors in psychology, arts, consumer services, and recreation begin with earnings slightly above 40,000 dollars. Degrees in early childhood education, ethnic and civilization studies, and human services start under 40,000 dollars for African Americans. Unfortunately, 39 percent of African American students selected majors that would result in low-paying jobs. Clearly, for the African American, major selection is as important as attending college at all. College may not be for everyone, and skilled professions can be equally lucrative. Cosmetologists and skilled auto mechanics and carpenters typically earn salaries over 40,000 dollars, while plumbers earn an average salary over 50,000 dollars. The best earnings occur when the people in this field are highly skilled in their craft.

Although Du Bois and Washington may have disagreed about how and when African Americans could achieve equality, they were both correct that it would take education, skills, or both to make it happen. We must ensure that our African American youth understand that they can be successful in a skilled or learned profession. If they choose a college, they must be very selective of their majors, and if they don't want to go to college, they do have to acquire the skills necessary to achieve the highest earnings possible in their chosen field.

Missed Opportunities

I was working on one of my construction jobs today, and a young man came by to ask me if I needed any help. I would have given him something to do if I had a job for him. However, most people would not have. You see, although he seemed nice enough, he was holding up his sagging pants with one hand, wore a white sleeveless t-shirt, and had a ton of very visible tattoos. In short, he looked like a thug. And most people, no matter their race, won't even hire a thug to cut their grass.

I once knew of a young man who was trying to enlist in the military. Though he was qualified physically, the military was refusing to let him enlist because of the tattoos on his neck, hands, and face. His family had the entire church praying for him, and I prayed too. But I also felt a certain way about this situation. This young man should have been taught by his parents that certain types of haircuts, clothing, accessories, and especially tattoos can make it more difficult for a black man to find gainful employment. We especially need to be careful of visible tattoos, because they cannot be concealed or covered when placed in certain areas. We as parents also need to be mindful of the types of clothing and accessories, we allow our children to wear for school and otherwise. We could be easily giving a teacher, security guard, or police officer cause to profile our children because they fit a certain stereotypical description. I am not saying this is right. I know it is a double standard, and I am as sad and angry about it as you are. But this is the way the world works for us as black people, and we must be aware for our and for the sake of our children. Parents, talk to your children. Tell them what their hair, clothing, piercings, tattoos, and accessories might be saying about them. Let them know that they will need every advantage they can get in this world to succeed, and that they must do their part to make sure they do not miss opportunities for themselves.

How to Win in an Interview

Mastering the job interview can take a combination of the right personality, the right skill set, and the right answers. But beyond that, there is an unspoken language of nonverbal cues that could actually make or break your chances of landing your dream job. The art is to know the nonverbal language we speak and to use it to effectively communicate to our interviewers that we are the man or woman for the job.

The first thing that we should pay attention to is our physical appearance. Our dress, in an interview, should always be modest. We are not seeking to draw attention to ourselves by way of trendy fashion, non-traditional hairstyles, or excessive perfume or cologne. In some cases, perfume and cologne could actually ruin your chances of getting the job, by causing an allergic reaction. A growing number of people have debilitating allergies to strong scents of any kind, and wearing it could be looked upon as insensitive or rude. Women should also steer clear of excessive jewelry, nails, and makeup. While we should seek to look our best, excessive makeup could be seen as vain or even provocative. In addition, the presence of long nails is seen by many as an unwillingness to work. Long nails can slow down typing and create obstacles to lifting, writing, filing, and generally get things done. Don't let that fancy manicure drive down your chances of getting the job you desire.

The second important nonverbal cue is the use of personal body language. When in an interview, make sure that you are engaged in the conversation by making regular eye contact with the interviewer. Many don't know that the depth and tone of your voice are often determined by the quality of your sleep the night before. So, make sure that you are rested and alert. Never let on that an interview is "too early" or "too late" in the day, as it communicates that you are not used to a traditional work schedule. Also, surveys show that people view avoiding eye contact, wringing hands, or rubbing the back of the neck or head as a sign of lying. So, check yourself to make sure that you are using your nonverbal cues effectively.

When it is finally your turn to speak, make sure you put your best foot forward. When asked, list your positive aspects first. Use this time to play up your strengths and experiences in a humble and modest way. Never brag or celebrate yourself openly in an interview. In fact, look for something professional to compliment the interviewer about. Making others feel important is a great way to add value to the interview and leave an impression that will last. Humor can be valuable in an interview, but not too much, and never to bash or make fun of anyone or anything. You never know who you may be dealing with and what their personal situation is. Lastly, never avoid a question in an interview. If you are not sure how to answer, it is ok to ask for clarification from the interviewer. Also, if you do not know the answer, be honest about it, while making sure to add something positive such as your experience in a related area or your willingness to learn. Even if you stumble, get back up, and run strong to the end. Your family's future is worth you giving the interview all you've got.

Landing the job you want, in this day and age, is going to take more than submitting a resume. You must come to the interview ready to win. Begin by making sure you are dressed for success. Cut the hair and nails if you need to. Take off the trendy eyelashes and nose ring. Visible tattoos are a turn-off for many. And I will say this again. Pull your pants up and wear a belt. No matter how qualified you are for the job, you may lose before you even open your mouth if your appearance paints a negative image in your interviewer's mind. Secondly, pay attention to your demeanor. Make sure your eye contact, posture, and voice depict you as competent, confident, and ready to win. Lastly, play up your strengths. Be honest about your experiences and leave value on the table. Your interviewers should walk away with that *good feeling* that leads to the callback and the contract. So much of this process is up to you, so make sure you apply the principles of interviewing that set you up for success!

Proverbs 3:5-6: *Trust in the Lord with all your heart, and do not lean on your own understanding. In all your ways acknowledge him, and he will make straight your paths.*

Making the Right Decisions when Buying a Car

I have heard people in conversations say something that makes very little sense to me. I have heard them say, "I will always have a car payment." This is because they trade their cars in every two or three years or sooner. Sometimes they even lease a car because the payments will be cheaper. Now I know a lot of businesspeople lease cars so that they can deduct the car, gas, and other maintenance from their taxes or their income. But it doesn't quite make the same sense for poor people to lease a car. It makes more sense for them to buy a car, pay for it for three or four years, and then drive it for five or six additional years—or in my case, twenty.

Don't be fooled by salesman from the dealership who sold you your last car and who keeps calling you to tell you to come in and look at the new cars every couple of years. Cars are not really an investment, and you should not treat them as if they are.

Do your homework before you purchase a car. When looking for a new or used car, there are things you should never do. Never walk into a showroom and tell the salesperson that you don't care how much the car costs as long as your payments are not more than 400 dollars a month. Never feel like you have it made because you are a teacher, a fireman, or a businessman. That is what you do all day every day, but the fact is that you do not do these types of negotiations on your job. If you are a woman who can take care of yourself, it still may not hurt to take a man with you as this may stop that salesperson from making many unimportant statements like how powerful the engine is and how fast the car will go. This could be a very nice person sitting in front of you, but you must remember that he is still a salesperson trained to take advantage of people every day.

Before you go to purchase that car, you must do your homework and have a general idea about the price of the car you are looking to buy. You should never agree to the price immediately. You must be firm about what you are willing to pay for the car. The salesperson may pretend to negotiate with you by taking your offer and going off to talk to a supervisor, but more than likely he will just go to get a glass of water since he already knows how low he can go for the car you desire. When he returns, he may say that he can only go so far and ask you to raise your price. Beware, while you are thinking, he will remind you of how limited the car is and what a great deal it is. He will tell you that this is the best deal you can possibly get. Unfortunately, if you go when you are tired or have a lot of other things to do, you may accept his offer as the best you can get. After meeting with the salesman, they will turn you over to another person who will tell you that you need undercoating to protect the bottom of the car from rusting out. They may also say that you need paint treatment that will protect the paint on the car. This person will tell you that all of this may cost 1,500 dollars but they will allow you to have it for a mere 900 dollars. Please understand that if the car you are purchasing is two years old or less, the previous owner probably already purchased this treatment.

Your next stop is the finance man, and he will have a few things up his sleeve as well. He may tell you that you did not qualify for the lowest financing but that he gave you the best interest he could. The next conversation will be about an extended warranty even though you may still have a year of warranty already on the car. He may then tell you that he can add two additional years for a low cost.

By the time this is all over, you have now surpassed the price you had intended to pay. The lesson is that you must ensure that everyone understands that what you intend to pay including everything else will not exceed what you intended to pay originally.

Proverbs 22:16: *He that oppresseth the poor to increase his riches, and he that giveth to the rich, shall surely come to want.*

Why You Should Buy a Tiny House

That is not just a tiny house. It is the beginning of big dreams fulfilled. It is somebody's home. Perhaps you should buy it. Your friends will laugh, but the joke will be on them. In the end, you will own a piece of the American dream, and they will continue to make their landlords rich. I know what you are saying. This is not your dream home. But before you count this idea out, consider how it could help you get there.

We have to start somewhere, and this is a good place to begin. This house could be yours in a short time. You would have all the tax and credit benefits of home ownership. You would also have a small mortgage payment that could give you a chance to pay off credit cards, student loans, or a car note. And unlike the average homeowner, you could feasibly pay this house off in much shorter than a thirty-year time frame. Then it would be yours to sell or trade and move up. My favorite suggestion would be that you keep it after you own it and rent it out for extra income. Let me tell you from experience that this would be better than a part-time job. Take the extra money and use it to buy another tiny house or perhaps a condo, townhome, or even a duplex to rent out to those same friends who laughed at your tiny-house idea a few years back. Before you know it, you will have made enough to purchase a third property. Just remember that no matter what your friends say, you can do this.

This idea is better than the stock market, better than mutual funds, and better than savings accounts. The banks are holding your money and lending it out to smart people who are using it to invest in themselves and their families. Furthermore, the banks are paying you next to nothing in interest for the use of your money. They are, however, charging a great deal of interest to their borrowers. They are thereby making money for themselves, all the while making you think they are helping you save yours.

This is something that I believe, and I want to bring this point around full circle: if you want to get ahead, you will have to be willing to go the extra mile. Remember that we need to follow the money, and the money is at the top. We will never become a lender by being content to be a borrower. We need to put effort into finding out how we can reach lender status. The good news for most people is that buying a home will ultimately be the best investment you make for your family over a lifetime. In the long term, real estate values increase and a mortgage can provide you with some level of financial security and a roof over your head, while also providing a stable place for your family to call home. At the end of the day, having something is better than having nothing. If this is idea is

not for you, then who is it for? And if this idea is not for you

now, then when? You will not be young forever, and it is time

to take a drastic step to start building your future. If not, you

may find yourself kicking that same tin can down the street for

the next five, ten, or twenty years. It is time for you to do

something different. People say all the time that they are young

and have plenty of time. I say to you that you are not that

young and you do not know how much time you have. Use

your time wisely.

Bankruptcy

Don't let people tell you that the best thing to do is file

bankruptcy and start over. Bankruptcy will be with you for a

very long time. In fact, every time you fill out a credit

application, you will be asked if you have ever filed

bankruptcy. Even certain job applications reserve the right to

run your credit and may even ask you explicitly if you have

ever filed bankruptcy. In essence, creditors want to know that

you have not given up on paying your debts.

Chapter 7 bankruptcy, which is total bankruptcy, stays on your credit report for ten years. Chapter 13 is more like a payment plan and will stay on your credit report for seven years. Do not believe what the bankruptcy lawyers tell you. It will not just make everything go away. Additionally, it just might make matters worse for you.

If You Carry Cash, You Spend Less

It is just too easy to hand the salesperson your credit card without counting the actual cost of what you are spending. Sometimes, we don't even think about it. But if you were paying in cash, and your actual green money was leaving your wallet and going into the salesperson's hands, you would think twice before you let that money leave your hands. Your hard-earned money is valuable, and swiping a card lets you part with it without feeling the consequence until later. Some people say they don't carry cash for safety reasons. Well, nowadays, cash is safer than plastic. If someone steals your cash, it is done and over, but if someone steals your credit card, they could use it to steal the money in your bank account, ruin your credit, and even steal your identity, causing you trouble for many years to come. You may think your money is safe because you have overdraft protection. Well, you will pay the bank to use that service with interest. Are you worried about the crooks on the street robbing you? What about the crooks at the bank?

Why Save

There are a lot of people who have no problem making money, but they have a big problem with keeping and saving their money. They will have to change their way of thinking. One problem that people have is that they try to look like they have money. They want to dress well, drive expensive cars, and buy big houses. The other problem is that people think there is always more where their money came from. They have no problems spending because, in their minds, they will keep their job and simply go back to work. Right? Wrong. People with these mindsets maintain a rhythm of work, spend, work, spend, repeat. When they have extra money, they do not know what to do with it. What about the future? What about when you retire at half salary? What if someone gets sick and you have to miss work to take care of them, or hire someone to care for them? What about your own health? One crisis could happen, and money will leak away from you like water from a faucet.

How to Save

Everybody wants to make a million dollars. But the way to make a million dollars is one dollar at a time. We need to ask ourselves the hard questions. How much money do I need so that I am not cash negative at the end of the month? You may need to cut back on some of your expenses. Failing to save is always a losing bet. Stop taking bets you cannot afford to lose.

You will need a strategy, but be careful. Utilize trusted sources. There are countless books, speakers, and TV shows that preach the value of starting a business and having money for the future. A few of those guys became millionaires from their own businesses. However, many of them became millionaires by selling books and tapes and by getting you to come to their seminars. If I could get you to come to my seminar where I sell dirt as they are not making any more dirt, I would be rich. So, find a trusted strategy that works for you. Put something away out of every paycheck. Research bank programs and investment programs sponsored by your job that may match your investments and help your money grow faster.

Set short-term and long-term goals and learn to live past today.

How to Get Out of Debt

The key is motivation, and that's more important than

math. The steps toward debt elimination may be as hard as

nailing Jell-O to a tree, but it can be done. It is a mind over

matter thing. Getting out of debt will require you to list all of

your debts in order, from the smallest to the largest. The plan is

not to pay more each month on as many bills as possible. The

plan is to take the smallest bill and pay as much as you can on

it until you pay it off. We begin with the smallest bill so that

we can see some success quickly and stay motivated. Then you

take the money you were using to pay that bill and apply it to

the next smallest bill. Repeat this strategy for the next bill.

Remember, nobody said this would be easy. It is a sacrifice.

But if you keep this in mind, getting out of debt can cease to be

a dream and actually become a reality.

Retirement

Many people say that they cannot afford to put money

away for retirement. This is what I have to say: you cannot

afford not to put money away for retirement. You need to put a little away each month if you are at all able. You have to keep in mind that social security was never meant to be your retirement. It was meant to be a supplement. Even with a below-average income, you still need to find a way to work on retirement. One way to do this is to not be concerned with the Joneses and what they have. I was watching TV the other day and Charlie Rose was interviewing a politician from China. He said, "Americans worry too much about China. Do you know what the Chinese worry about? China." I think that, in some ways, we black people worry too much about the Joneses and other people when we should be worried about ourselves. We cannot put our eggs in one basket and assume that social security will be there for us when we retire. And even if it is there, it will not be enough.

You Need a Will

Statistics tell us 70 percent of Americans will die without a will. That's dumb. If one thing is certain, it is death. Why would you die and leave your family and friends fighting over money and things? Or worse yet, why would you have the state decide what will happen to your money, home, and other belongings? A man must always have a level head. Well, what's in your head now? Rocks? Get a will, dummy, and don't make your family go to court fighting over your two dollars.

You can't get out of a hole by digging out the bottom.

—Elmo Overton

Sell some of your stuff and make your broke friends question your sanity.

—Elmo Overton

Proverbs 3:5-6: *Trust in the Lord with all of your heart and do not lean on your own understanding. In all your ways acknowledge Him, and He will make your paths straight.*

It is Time to Move Up

We have too many people who are cleaning the office, but not enough people who are office managers. We have too many people who want to work in the house, but not enough people who want to design and draw blueprints for the house. We have too many people who want to work as electricians, plumbers, and on heating and cooling machines, but not enough people who want to own and run the company. Some want to change this, but somebody has to take action. Talking will not always be the answer.

Joshua 1:9: *Remember that I have commanded you to be determined and confident! Do not be afraid or discouraged, for I, the Lord your God, am with you wherever you go.*

Why You Should Pack Up and Move

The cities of East Saint Louis, Illinois; Detroit, Michigan; Chicago, Illinois; and New Orleans, Louisiana, have all been listed as some of the most violent cities in the United States. The combination of abject poverty and a desperate economy have taken their tolls on these cities, leaving the inhabitants in conditions that rival Third World countries. One Detroit resident writes, "I tell you this much, Chicago is a vacation place for people in Detroit. You will see, the whole city is being abandoned. Whole buildings, police stations with their computers on the floor and chairs being decayed, post offices, schools, whole blocks leveled to the ground. There are about 50 thousand street dogs, most of them pit bulls. Recently jackals have been reported. 3 out of 5 is a ruined house. You can't say you've been to Detroit just because you drive down 75 or 94. I tell you this much, you will never ever go to a gas station in Detroit, ever. Every school has a metal detector, like you are going into a cell. It's a mess really. It's a shame. It was the best city in the world just 60 years ago, had the highest job ranking and even to these days American economy depends on this city. By the way according to real statistics released by government officials METRO DETROIT has been #1 the most dangerous metropolitan cities in the USA for 10 years in a row."

While there are some common threads that link the most dangerous cities, there are also some outliers that are rarely discussed in the news. If we've heard it once, we've heard it a million times. Low-income areas are more prone to violent crime than middle- or high-income areas. But why is this? According to Sam Sieber of 24/7 Wall St. magazine, "A well-educated population tends to be more prosperous and less violent. In eight of the ten most dangerous states, education attainment rates are below the national average." So, we see here that it is not only the lack of income that makes certain areas more prone to crime, but also perhaps the lack of opportunity or skills to obtain gainful employment that create an environment where crime can run rampant. Perhaps the problem is that in areas where the schools and the economy have failed the children, the streets become the teachers and crime becomes the institute of higher learning.

Now let's discuss the outliers. Did you know that, in 2016, Alaska was number one in the country for incidences of violent crime? Here we have neither poverty, nor a lack of education, yet incidences of rape are highest of anywhere in the country. What we do have is a state where men outnumber women by the highest margin in the country.

Also, we can see from our list of the most dangerous states in the country that many of the areas hit hardest by crime are some of our country's most "touristy" places. States like Florida, Louisiana, Tennessee, and Washington, DC, made the list of the country's most violent states, with all but DC landing in the top ten. It is important to note that where there are densely populated areas, there is a trend toward crime. Tourists often fall prey to those who take advantage of the fact that people are carrying money, unaware of their surroundings, and will often relax their standards in the name of a good time.

Thirdly, the majority of violent crimes in this country is not murder, but aggravated assault. These numbers often go hand in hand with robbery or rape attempts.

Because of the world we live in, crime and violence will always be a part of life. However, my question is, why would you stay in an area where there are no jobs, failing schools, and so much crime? Why would you let your children attend a school that spends more money on metal detectors than books? Why not pack up what you have and start over someplace else? Many people fear leaving the places that are familiar to them. However, this fear may be keeping you from a better life for you and your children. There are places you can go where crime is lower, and the chances for a better life through education and opportunity are greater. Don't be afraid to take that chance.

1 Thessalonians 4:11-12: *And to aspire to live quietly, and to mind your own affairs, and to work with your hands, as we instructed you, so that you may walk properly before outsiders and be dependent on no one.*

Money + Politics = Power

The people with money support the politics of those who support them and their agenda, and the people with the money have no problem telling the politician that if they do not support their policies and them, they will give their money to the opponents. But the problem may be, who is supporting the little guy with a lot of dreams for himself and his family? In this country, everything rolls downhill, and if you are at the bottom, you will catch it. The money will go to money-hungry CEOs and big bank credit card companies, just to name a few. They will reap all of the benefits. As a matter of fact, these CEOs and other unbalanced areas of wealth took in 80 percent of the worth in this country. Even with this, they continue to go back for more. It's almost like giving red meat to a lion that will just get him started. The rich always seem to get richer, and the poor always seem to get poorer.

Where Are We Now?

We have come a long way since slavery, since Jim Crow, since segregation. But where are we now? Are we still pushing as hard as we once did, or have we slacked up some? Are too many of us still walking around saying, "I am doing alright" and "Don't worry, be happy"? As for myself, I was doing alright when we were living in the projects eating beans three times a week sometimes. But the fact is that we need to do better than alright. Why can't we do good or better? There are people walking around saying that we are where we are because we don't work hard enough or that we don't know what to do with the money we make. I call all of that garbage. A lot of us have worked hard enough to get to the door of success and have been knocked down, knocked back, and have had doors slammed in our faces. We do not have the luxury of having grandfathers or fathers that can bankroll us or give us a job. Very few of our African American families have a history of affluence or influence.

Furthermore, we as a community have been reluctant to put our money together to purchase shopping centers, hotels, apartment complexes, doctors' offices, and law firms. These are the businesses we should be striving to own because it puts us in a position to employ other qualified individuals in our own communities. Don't get me wrong—we have all those things, but we need more.

We need more people to put their money together toward a common goal. We all talk, but we need more people to put their money where their mouth is.

Our greatest weapon against poverty, systemic racism, and underemployment is education. We have to see to it that our children are receiving the best education possible from the very beginning. If our children are in a school that cannot pass the minimum requirements for the state, then it is our responsibility to take them out and put them in another school. We must be willing to take matters into our own hands. The teachers and principals can be as nice as they want to be, but if they are giving our children a subpar education, they are not doing them any good. Another weapon we have is unity in our own community. That means we should own the corner store, nail salon, barber shop, and restaurants in our communities as well as the buildings that house them. Unity means that those of us who are in positions of power should seek to help others get ahead.

My friends and I who are building houses are seeking to train others who want to get into the building business for free, and to help them in any way we can. Also, those of us who are aspiring to achieve success should seek out and reach out for internships, apprenticeships, and opportunities to learn from those who are already doing it and have succeeded.

We've all heard of the good ole boy system. These are the circles where power is kept amongst those lucky enough to be a part of the system or know someone who is. Other minorities have a form of this same system where they help one another by spending money together, patronizing one another, and hiring their own. The African American community has the ability to do just that and to promote from within. We can create our system for our own boys and girls.

For those of us who say we work better by ourselves and don't need any help, my question is, how is that working out for you? You may have a big head, but two heads are still better than one. The more hands working toward a common goal, the better. Now let's get this job done and go home.

Are We starting Our Children Out Too Soon?

These are just my thoughts, but it seems to me that we as a community immerse our children in culture too soon. And by doing so, we send them a message that being cool is more important than spirituality, education, and old-fashioned hard work.

Perhaps we are starting our children out too early with designer label clothes, trendy haircuts, and popular culture. We've all seen it: the newborn babies with the 100-dollar tennis shoes, the toddlers that have perfected the latest dance moves, and the young child who knows every lyric to the popular rap songs. We've seen the children who know the life story behind their favorite sports icon or music idol. We have seen our young people obsessed with designer brands so much that their parents go into debt to make clothing purchases. We have even seen the public-school systems in many of our nation's most vulnerable areas switch to uniform policies in an attempt to solve this problem of clothing covetousness.

Perhaps the most tragic evidence that this problem exists lies in the countless cases of kids, teens, and young adults who have entered into lives of drug dealing and other illegal activities, trying to live the "high life" they see on TV and music videos.

Perhaps these children and young people do not know the real secret to life. And perhaps it is our fault as parents. Perhaps we subconsciously set them up for failure. It is all in what we expose them to. It is the lie of culture. The truth is that without the benefit of maturity and leadership, the world will lie to our children. Magazine articles, music, and entertainment all say, in various ways, that the way you look and dress is everything. And there are very educated marketers and PR personnel at every turn of this entertainment industry who are paid very well to create and perpetuate this myth. However, the truth is that most people have what they have because they work hard for it. Even the movie stars, actors, and musicians we see on TV work very hard to make what they do look easy. The truth is that, without a good education, you will be very limited in your career choices and your income potential. The real truth is, without God, even if you achieve the world's success, your life will be empty.

We need to teach these truths to our kids before we expose them to the culture's destructive lies. We need to let them see that the majority of people making top dollar in this world could not care less about wearing 300-dollar shoes. We need to tell them about the so-called "nerds" that we went to school with who are now presidents of companies and millionaires in their various fields. We need to teach them first that their foundation must be to place their trust in God. Instead of rap lyrics, our children should be learning scriptures that will benefit them in life and give them tools to tackle the hardships that will inevitably come. Secondly, we need to teach our children that education is the ticket to take them anywhere they want to go in life. We need to expose them to doctors, and lawyers, and engineers, and business owners, and non-traditional fields such as contracting, web designing, and political science. We need to look for where their strengths lie and encourage them to pursue fields that match their gifts and interests. We need to turn off the TV and have candid conversations with our kids. We should be honest with them, letting them know that college is not for everyone, but that some form of education is for everyone. We should let our children know that mechanics, hairstylists, and truck drivers can make a great living as long as they run their business with integrity and professionalism. These are the things our kids desperately need to know before they are exposed to the rappers and "housewives" that will paint a very different picture. With the tools of a Godly perspective, respect for education, and knowledge of the necessity of hard work, our children will be better able to navigate the lies of popular culture without becoming caught up in the hype.

Our children deserve to hear the truth from the people they look up to and respect. It is the parents' responsibility to give their children a fighting chance in this world by telling them the truth about the potential traps that could snare them and keep them from success. We would do well to turn off the TV when our kids come home from school, and make their knowledge of God, education, and hard work our top priority.

Fight the Good Fight

Let's face it. In this world, you will have your own personal Goliath standing right in front of you. Now what? You will have your problems and you will say to yourself, "What's going on here? I am reading my Bible daily and I am all prayed up." But you need to know something. You will have relationship problems, financial problems, health problems, and legal problems, but that does not mean that those problems have you. We can't let our problems dictate our character.

We will have to fight to handle some of the problems we face. When it is time to fight, you will have to get down in the trenches. There is mud and dirt in the trenches. Those of us who have been in the military know that you put the fighting people in front. The leaders are the ones who stand in the back and plan how the fight should go. Everybody knows this. But if this is the way it is done in a real battle, why do we, as blacks, put our civil rights leaders in the front while the army is in the rear, in many cases, doing nothing?

What about the reverse Robin Hood tactics that black people disproportionately fall prey to? Predatory lending of many kinds seeks to rob the poor and make the lenders rich. How could these schemes still be legal?

Some would say that people need to pay closer attention to the fine print on the financial agreements they sign. This may be true. But we should be fighting to change some of these laws. It is not good enough to be legally right. Things need to be morally right. Legal people will cut your head off and hand it to you and say, "This is not personal; it's just business." The law in this great country allows people to do almost anything and justify it by saying it is legal. Sometimes hard-working people get the short end of the stick because someone did something wrong to another person and the law allowed it.

What about poverty? This is a problem every black person in America should be fighting to overcome. There are many blacks and whites alike that refuse to try and help the poor because they say that government programs such as welfare, food stamps, and Section 8 housing are designed to aid the poor. But most hard-working people would much prefer a job that pays a fair wage over a government handout. What is funny and sad to me is to hear people who make a decent salary say that the working poor are poor because they don't work hard enough. Many of these people grew up poor themselves, but now have money and are too good to reach back to help others.

Let me say this right now. I am blessed, grateful, and humble for what I have. God has blessed me and my family. We have more than we need. All of my children have advanced degrees. But while I call myself blessed; I am not content. I still work because not only do I want to help myself, but others who are not doing well. These people are not just my family. Most of them are people I have not yet met. I tell young people all the time not to spend their money on renting any longer than they have to. Especially for married men, my advice is to purchase a home. A man should pay himself with his mortgage instead of spending his life making his landlord rich. I know some people that have very nice clothes, a new car in the garage, and the best of furniture, all in a house that is rented. We do not need to eat the crumbs from someone else's table. No. We need to own the house, the table, the food, and the crumbs. I also tell them to stop spending their money on material things in stores that they don't need. Anyone who loves to spend money in the stores should take some of that stuff back to the store and ask for a loan against these items. Ask the man to loan you some of the money that you have spent there for all these years. Just stand right there and wait for security to come. That man will think that you are crazy, when in actuality, you simply made a bad investment. Here is the hard question. What about you? Do you think that you will in some ways always eat the crumbs off the master's table, so you settle for nice clothes and a fancy car? Stop thinking like that and think higher. You may look really good but you come really cheap.

Whatever Happened to the Village?

The Group "Fire" sung these words in their song "It takes a Village":

"Whatever happened to 'It takes a village to raise a child'?

Whatever happened to 'Save the children cause they've gone wild'?

Do you know the future is in?

The lives of children?

Bring back those days of love."

This song, derived from an ancient African proverb, denotes the importance of community influence in the lives of children.

Lawrence Mbogoni, an African professor, wrote: "Proverb or not, 'It takes a whole village to raise a child' reflects a social reality some of us who grew up in rural areas of Africa can easily relate to. As a child, my conduct was a concern of everybody, not just my parents, especially if it involved misconduct. Any adult had the right to rebuke and discipline me and would make my mischief known to my parents who in turn would also meet their own 'punishment'. The concern of course was the moral well-being of the community."

This sentiment has been echoed by numerous politicians and activists in the attempts to foster hope and forward mobility for struggling communities and people groups. But what is the village? Who are its members? And why has it ceased to exist?

Know Better Do Better

I think the important thing to know is that modern people do not live in villages. Most of us live in diverse communities that encompass a vast variety of cultures, beliefs, and value systems. How, then, can the villages we now live in be integral to the well-being of our children?

But there was a time not too long ago when black people had a community all of their own. Shared neighborhoods, schools, jobs, transportation, and churches fostered a community where people became invested in the lives of others. Whether they were family or not was not important. People looked out for each other. They learned of needs and interjected themselves into the equations of others. Children in the black community not only had the benefit of their natural parents, but also the benefit of pastors, teachers, community activists, cousins, aunts, uncles, and friends.

However, as the black community evolved, many dreamed of leaving it in hopes of fostering a "better" life for their children. This often meant removing children from the communities of their parents and placing them in communities that did not recognize them. Meanwhile, those who stayed in the communities were faced with the task of working with a shell of the community that once was, and an overwhelming inability to strike a balance between the wholesome and the unhealthy. At the end of the day, both, those who left and those who stayed, were left with an identity problem and a lack of healthy community in either place.

So now that we know what happened to the village, how do we get it back for the sake of ourselves and our children? We must rebuild them. Our communities must now be an intentional act of each individual to find and foster relationships with mentors, mentees, advisers, coaches, and friends. We all need a support system, because no one can be successful alone. Everyone from the corporate CEO to the stay-at-home mom needs some kind of a support system. Just like the villages of the African proverb, we all thrive better in the company of others who are all striving toward a common goal. To quote Julian Gordon, founder of masterminds.org, "Success is not a matter of time. It is a matter of team."

Find your village.

Destiny

Destiny is everything that happens to you in your life and after that. Your destiny equates to what is meant to happen in your life. For example, you may want to be president, a senator, or a business owner. You may be destined for greatness in this area, and it very well may be your calling to pursue this position. Still, if this is your destiny, you will have to work for it. You will have to labor and pay your dues. You will have to campaign and politicize. You will have to save money and invest it wisely. You will have to stay focused and overcome obstacles, distractions, and setbacks. Your destiny will not just happen. You will have to prepare yourself for greatness and be ready when the opportunity presents itself.

There is a story about a farmer who prayed for a bountiful harvest. So, the Lord gave him everything he needed to produce this harvest. The farmer was blessed with seed, land, physical strength, skill, and the perfect amounts of rain and sunshine. But still the farmer stayed in his house praying for a great crop. His destiny was never realized because he never worked his field. He had everything he needed and it was time for him to go to work. There are a lot of things that are given to us. All we need to do is go get it.

True story

I know a man named Raymond who worked as a demolition contractor. Raymond worked for a small company tearing down houses and small commercial buildings. However, Raymond had dreams of one day owning his own construction company. Among the small demolition companies, there is fierce competition, e xcept when there is a large job about to be sold for demolition. During those times, the smaller companies know how to come together and pool their resources together to bid corporately for the larger jobs. Oftentimes, the general contractors will give their jobs to the smaller companies with the stipulation that they have at least ten dump trucks, four front loaders, and two heavy equipment machines for tearing down buildings. After the job is done, the small companies go their separate ways. Raymond took these opportunities to put his best foot forward, show his best work efforts, and make connections with the other contracting staff heads.

One day, the owner of company A called the owner of company B and said that he will need to take an extended leave of absence owing to illness. He asked for one of his dependable, experienced persons to help run the business in his absence, and Raymond's name was mentioned. With his boss's blessing, he began to learn the ropes of business management and ownership at this new company. One day the owner of this company called Raymond into his office and said that he will no longer be able to run his business. He must concentrate on trying to get better and not on running a company. He was interested in selling the business. The business owner worked out a deal where Raymond would lease the building, and the owner would finance the business for five years. Because of Raymond's hard work, all parties were confident that Raymond could keep the business running and even grow the business exponentially.

Now six months ago, Raymond was a truck driver, heavy equipment operator, and laborer. It was not a bad job, and Raymond could have been content driving trucks for the rest of his life. However, Raymond took his destiny into his own hands and faithfully worked hard to achieve it. Now Raymond is a company president.

Moving Forward after Tragedy: Lucy McBath

Lucy McBath worked as a flight attendant for Delta Airlines for thirty years. She is a two-time breast cancer survivor, wife, and mother. She is active in her church, and in her sorority.

Lucy comes from a family of black activists. Her father was the president of the Illinois chapter of the NAACP and served on the national board. Her mother was a registered nurse who tutored others in how to pass their nurse's exams.

Lucy was a good mother. She was involved in her son Jordan's life and education. She homeschooled him for a time because her neighborhood school was a Title 1 failing school and she did not want him to attend there. She released him to return to public school where she supported his participation in the Air Force ROTC with aspirations to enter the Air Force after graduation. She monitored where he went and the company he kept. She taught him how to keep himself safe, and had hard conversations with him about what it means to be young and black. She discussed the Trayvon Martin case with her son, and prayed for him to have wisdom in times when he was out in the world alone.

But nothing could have prepared Lucy for November 23, 2012, when her son's father called to say that their son Jordan had been fatally shot at a convenience store by a forty-seven-year-old White man who objected to the music he was playing in his car. It was the day after Thanksgiving, and Jordan had gone Christmas shopping with friends. Apparently, the man asked Jordan and his friends to turn down the music, and Jordan refused. The shooter then shot ten times into the car, fatally wounding seventeen-year-old Jordan. The shooter claimed that the teens had a gun and had threatened to kill him, yet no gun was ever found in Jordan's car. This shooting sparked national protests and a public outcry against racism, gun violence, and black pariahdom. Still, this senseless crime took over two years and two trials to bring the shooter to justice. At the first trial, the shooter, Michael Dunn, was convicted of three counts of attempted murder, but was not convicted of the first-degree murder of Jordan Davis until a retrial two years later.

Lucy's grief saw a ray of hope that day. She was grateful that justice had been served for her son. But it was not enough for her to go home and tend to her own grief. Something inside her said that she was the one who needed to fight for the nameless, faceless mothers and children all over this country whose lives have been shattered by gun violence, never to be mended. Those whose faces were not in the paper, whose stories were never told, and whose killers were never brought to justice. Lucy decided that she would be the one to speak up. In an interview with CNN, McBath stated, "It's just not enough to have the marches and the rallies and the speeches and the remarks. Championing for them in Washington is still championing for my child, I'm still a mother, I'm still parenting. That's why I believe this was the time to stand up."

McBath began to work with an organization called Everytown for Gun Safety. She spoke at rallies, petitioned in Washington, and encouraged the public to get involved. She actively campaigned for Hillary Clinton as one of the "Mothers of the Movement" whose children had been killed by police brutality or gun violence. She became the spokesperson of Moms Demand Action for Gun Sense in America. She began to fight against "stand your ground" laws. And now, five years after her son's murder, Lucy McBath ran for and won the Democratic primary for the sixth congressional district seat in the US House of Representatives. This is a seat that has not been held by a Democrat since 1979, and has never been held by a woman.

McBath intends to use her life experiences to platform for the issues she cares about. As a mother who lost her son to gun violence, she will fight for gun restrictions. McBath is adamant that she is not an anti-gun candidate. According to her campaign, McBath wants background checks for all gun sales, the defeat of conceal-carry reciprocity, a higher minimum-age-of-purchase, and laws that ban domestic abusers and criminals from buying guns.

She wants to see tougher restrictions placed on those who are previous offenders or mentally ill. In an interview with ABC News, McBath stated, "The thing about it is that I'm not against guns. I'm not against the Second Amendment. I'm not against law-abiding gun owners and hunters owning their guns." What she is against, she said, is people who "want to use their guns in a way that is criminal."

As a breast cancer survivor, McBath will seek to uphold the Affordable Care Act and will also use her educational experiences with her son to seek more funding for Georgia K-12 public schools. McBath also states that since she knows what it is like to have her family torn apart, she will fight to keep families from being torn apart by immigration.

In a recent interview, McBath told ABC News, "I never expected (any of) this to happen, but I know that in light of all my experiences, to not to do anything is a tragedy in itself." Let's stand behind this candidate and others like her who are moving forward despite adversity and seeking to make a better day for the generations to come.

God has a destiny for all of us even if we don't know or understand it. When David was a boy attending his father's flock, do you think he ever thought he would become a fierce fighter, and leader of men, not to mention a king? But God had a destiny for King David. God was working out David's destiny all along. David only needed to work hard and be ready when the opportunity presented itself.

No matter how devastating our present situation may be, God's resources are infinite. No matter what our economic situation, if we believe and work hard, we can achieve the destiny God has for us. In the book of Ruth, when Ruth worked in the fields, do you think she knew that she would marry Boaz and would own that very field and more? Maybe not. But Ruth showed kindness to her mother-in-law and worked hard in Boaz's field. God positioned her perfectly and gave her Boaz's favor. Sometimes we don't know what our destiny will be, but faith and hard work can position us for greatness.

In the book of Esther, Esther was a poor Jewish girl who was so beautiful that she won the affection of the king more than any other woman. So, the king set a royal crown on her head and made her queen instead of Vashti, the old queen. Then when Esther found out that Haman had a plan to kill and annihilate the Jews, Esther went to the king to beg for her life and the lives of all the Jews. Esther's destiny had been set long ago. The favor she had gotten of the king was no accident. This favor would be much needed when it was time for action. She was to use it to save the Jewish people.

Someone asked me if I am my brother's keeper, and the answer is yes. I am. If I am able to help my brother in any way, I should try to help them. Who knows whether the opportunity I give him will get him one step closer to where he was destined to be. People think that where they are in life is permanent. It is not. You can come down just like you went up, and it is important to reach back to help others if you can. I tell my kids that their feet are already too big for my shoes because they are standing on my shoulders. They have never lived in the projects, never worked the kinds of jobs I had to work, and never had to start from rock bottom. My dreams, aspirations, and hopes are that they would not start from where I am now, but would go to a good college and get a degree. Then they can start from there. And now, I have the same hopes for my grandchildren, that they would go even further in college and start there. That is what I am shooting for. Now I don't believe that a four-year college is for everyone, but I do believe that some kind of training after high school is a must. Local college, junior college, vocational school, or any kind of training in electrical, plumbing, framing, contracting, or any skilled trade can get you where you want to be in life if you are willing to believe and work hard. I know some tradesmen who make more than teachers, public administrators, and many other graduate-level positions. But if you think that all you need is a high school diploma to go out and fight the world, you are wrong. The world will do you in fast. It is your destiny to do the very best you can.

Money is not everything. It is temporary. But you do need money to live in America. Money does not equate to success. Success is forever. God is the source of both money and success, and oftentimes hard work and preparation are the only things that can help us achieve both. Go get your destiny.

Chapter Four

Prayer is the Answer

I believe the American dream is still alive, and it is imperative that we stand on the side of right without worrying about those who you feel may be on the side of wrong. We need to be prepared to help those who are less fortunate than we are and those who for a variety of reasons may be down on their luck. We must be prepared to fight for equality, fight for fairness, and, most importantly, fight for those who are unable to fight for themselves.

Oftentimes, it is hard to determine the best way to help others. The first step is to seek wisdom and guidance from God. Understanding God's desire for us allows us to know that our purpose in life is to pray for the wisdom to make the world a better place. When we are called to help our fellow man, we often stumble because of judgment. Judgment keeps us from helping others and leads us to blame the victim for their own circumstances. Prayer allows us to look past our judgments and to do what God would have us do. Like God himself, we are called to look past our own desires and put others before ourselves. While prayer shows us how to treat others, prayer also shows us how to treat ourselves.

Like those facing hardships, prayer can provide guidance for our lives even if we are not in crisis. I once heard someone say that people often use God like a spare tire. We seek him when we are in trouble but ignore him when everything is going smoothly. Those who really know the key to success understand that it requires an unfailing commitment to serving and seeking God's wisdom. As I conclude, I pray that this book provides encouragement to those who feel hopeless, courage to those who feel they are incapable of changing their circumstances, an understanding that poverty does not have to be inevitable, and a call to action to be better while doing better.

Imagine!

Close your eyes for a moment and imagine. What is your vision for your future? Where do you see yourself in five, ten, or twenty years? What are some challenges you would like to be done with? What are some good practices that you would like to continue? Here's a secret. The next five, ten, or twenty years are going to come and go whether you move forward with your plan or not. You could sit and let time pass with no progress, or you could plan for the future by doing what needs to be done now, to promote a better tomorrow. It's just like anything else. If you know what time you have to leave for work in the morning, you have to set your alarm clock to be up in time and get yourself ready. For some, that's an hour. Some people can get ready in as little as twenty minutes. But by now, you know how much time you need and (if you want to keep your job) you plan accordingly. The same goes for saving to meet goals. What if you want to pay off your car early? How much of an extra payment could you afford to make each month? How many months will it take to meet your goal? What would be your approximate month of payoff? Write it down, and keep it in front of you. We humans are forgetful, and if you don't keep your goals front and center, something else will demand attention. In this case, I will give you permission to be somewhat selfish. If you are truly committed to your goal, you may have to say no to otherwise good expenditures. You may have to reduce the amount you spend on restaurants. You may even have to pick up a few extra shifts a month and designate the money toward your goal. But here's the thing. Once you conquer a small giant in your life, you will have confidence to conquer a bigger one. You may decide, after paying off your car, to allocate that money toward the purchase of a new home, or you may decide to begin a college fund for your child. How much do you want to save? How much time do you have? Post your goal and keep it before you. Keep with it and be consistent. Repeat. Before you know it, with some hard work that you did for yourself, you could accomplish some of those dreams that before you had only imagined.

Jump!

Have you ever watched Double Dutch? The player who is about to jump into the ropes must first create a cadence that mimics the rhythm of the ropes. They do this to ready themselves before jumping in. But what would happen if the player continued to stand on the sidelines, readying themselves, and never jumped in? That player would eventually lose his or her turn to jump. Let's liken this to your life. Are you sitting on the sidelines? Are you ready to jump in, but instead continue to mimic the rhythms of those around you? Are you choosing to be a "turner" because you are afraid to jump in and fail? Whatever your chosen method of hesitation, it will all be for naught if you don't get out there and try. If you don't take your turn and start working toward the positive goals you have always wished for, it will never happen. Eventually it will be too late.

Of course, first you must put some thought into what you are going to do. What skills do you have? These skills don't always have to come from a classroom. Are you gifted at organization? Do you have a craft? Are you a people person? Do you have on-the-job experience that you could put to work for yourself? Do you know anyone who is fiscally responsible that you could talk to and devise a plan? Get out of the hesitation trap by using what is in your hands.

Next, you have to take a risk. Yes, failure is possible, but if you don't make an attempt to get ahead, you will certainly never get ahead. Success doesn't happen by accident. And what if you do fail? You are sure to learn something new, and what you learn could be the key to your success. You have spent your entire life building your boss's future. Your long hours, dedication, and dependability have helped build his company. You have to see your own future as worth the investment and worth the risk.

Finally, after you have decided to take action, devised a plan, and assumed the risk, you must take a deep breath, and jump. Launch that small business. Purchase that investment property. Offer that program. Teach that course. Execute that plan to secure a solid future for yourself and your family. Once we know better, we can all do better.